The Power of Conversation

I0888816

Powerful conversations facilitate powerful thinking. In *The Power of Conversation,* seasoned educator Barbara Kohm provides a roadmap for how to grow into a great leader and transform your schools. Designed for principals to harness the power of focused professional conversation, this book uses dialogues between principals and mentors or colleagues to explore everyday school dilemmas, such as scheduling, discipline, budgeting, and instruction. Each chapter explores transformational themes, provides strategies and guidelines for leaders to apply in their own schools, and includes reflective exercises. This book provides an accessible and thoughtful way for principals to talk about complicated issues, deepen their thinking, and develop the skills that fuel transformational leadership.

Barbara Kohm is a veteran principal, teacher, consultant, and mentor. She is the co-founder of the Clayton Family Center in Missouri.

Other Eye On Education Books

Available from Routledge
(www.routledge.com/eyeoneducation)

The Leader's Guide to Working with Underperforming Teachers: Overcoming Marginal Teaching and Getting Results
Sally J. Zepeda

The Principalship from A to Z, 2nd Edition
Ronald Williamson and Barbara R. Blackburn

School Leadership Through the Seasons: A Guide to Staying Focused and Getting Results All Year
Ann T. Mausbach and Kimberly Morrison

The Revitalized Tutoring Center: A Guide to Transforming School Culture
Jeremy Koselak and Brad Lyall

College for Every Student: A Practitioner's Guide to Building College and Career Readiness
Rick Dalton and Edward P. St. John

What Successful Principals Do! 199 Tips for Principals, 2nd Edition
Franzy Fleck

7 Ways to Transform the Lives of Wounded Students
Joe Hendershott

Five Critical Leadership Practices: The Secret to High-Performing Schools
Ruth C. Ash and Pat H. Hodge

Mentoring Is a Verb: Strategies for Improving College and Career Readiness
Russ Olwell

How to Make Data Work: A Guide for Educational Leaders
Jenny Grant Rankin

A School Leader's Guide to Implementing the Common Core: Inclusive Practices for All Students
Gloria Campbell-Whatley, Dawson Hancock, and David M. Dunaway

Hiring the Best Staff for Your School: How to Use Narrative to Improve Your Recruiting Process
Rick Jetter

BRAVO Principal! Building Relationships with Actions that Value Others, 2nd Edition
Sandra Harris

Get Organized! Time Management for School Leaders, 2nd Edition
Frank Buck

The Educator's Guide to Writing a Book: Practical Advice for Teachers and Leaders
Cathie E. West

The Power of Conversation

Transforming Principals into Great Leaders

Barbara Kohm

Routledge
Taylor & Francis Group
NEW YORK AND LONDON

First published 2017
by Routledge
711 Third Avenue, New York, NY 10017

and by Routledge
2 Park Square, Milton Park, Abingdon, Oxon, OX14 4RN

Routledge is an imprint of the Taylor & Francis Group, an informa business

Library of Congress Cataloging in Publication Data
Names: Kohm, Barbara, author.
Title: The power of conversation : transforming principals into great leaders / by Barbara Kohm.
Description: New York : Routledge, [2017]
Identifiers: LCCN 2016020509 | ISBN 9781138913912 (hardcover) | ISBN 9781138913929 (pbk.) | ISBN 9781315691145 (ebook) | ISBN 9781317429210 (mobipocket/kindle)
Subjects: LCSH: School principals--In-service training. | Educational leadership. | Mentoring in education.
Classification: LCC LB2831.9 .K65 2017 | DDC 371.2/012--dc23LC record available at https://lccn.loc.gov/2016020509

ISBN: 978-1-138-91391-2 (hbk)
ISBN: 978-1-138-91392-9 (pbk)
ISBN: 978-1-315-69114-5 (ebk)

Typeset in Optima
by Saxon Graphics Ltd, Derby

Contents

Meet the Author

Barbara Kohm has served as an early childhood program director, elementary school principal, consultant, mentor, and author. She is a co-founder of the Clayton Family Center that offers parenting classes and other child development services for parents and children from birth to five years old.

During her 14 years as principal of Captain Elementary School in St. Louis, Missouri, she transformed the curriculum and built a collaborative culture based on systems thinking. Applying those ideas and tools to the everyday life of teachers, students, and parents, she set in motion a process of continual growth and learning that raised test scores as well as morale. That experience is the basis of her writing and consulting.

As a mentor and coach, she's worked with principals to develop the deep thinking skills that outstanding leadership requires. A principal's job is so busy it often seems there is no time to think. Barbara believes that great leaders reverse this equation. They spend as much time thinking as doing. Structured conversations with coaches and like-minded colleagues can facilitate this process.

Barbara's previous publications include:

Barbara Kohm and Beverly Nance, *Principals Who Learn: Asking the Right Questions Seeking the Best Solutions* (Alexandria, VA: Association for Supervision and Curriculum Development, 2007).

Barbara Kohm and Beverly Nance, "Creating Collaborative Cultures," *Educational Leadership* 67(2): 67–72 (2009).

Barbara Kohm, "Improving Faculty Conversations," *Educational Leadership* 59(8): 31–33 (2002).

Barbara Kohm, "Choose Your Own Adventure," in *Schools That Learn* by Peter Senge et al. (New York, NY: Doubleday, 2000).

Preface

This book is designed to harness the power of focused professional conversation to grow principals into transformational leaders. Each chapter consists of conversations between principals and mentors, colleagues, or coaches that focus on the transformational ideas and practical suggestions that provide the structural foundation of great schools.

Why I Wrote the Book

From 2000 to the present, I served as mentor to principals who had strikingly different personalities and worked in a wide variety of settings. Despite these differences the most successful principals had many things in common. Most important, they worked with teachers to develop a supportive culture with high standards and a common focus. A synergy developed in their schools that enhanced each person's individual efforts and produced solid results. This success engendered a spirit of efficacy, optimism, and energy that enabled teachers to effectively engage in the complex work of meeting every student's learning needs. Conversations that helped principals develop these cultures are the focus of this book.

The principals I worked with needed opportunities to explore problems from a variety of viewpoints and evaluate them in the context of larger goals. They also needed time to explore the complex connections that weave together to create the learning experiences they provided their students.

The natural flow of conversation provides an opportunity to explore this complexity. The conversations move back and forth from the everyday details of a principal's life to the theoretical frameworks and ultimate goals that give meaning and direction to these details. And the subtle interplay between the wisdom of experience and the power of reflection enriches the dialogue. The book offers principals an entry into such conversations and mentors a model for developing conversations of their own.

For Whom I Wrote the Book

An obvious audience for these conversations is new and aspiring principals. However, the best principals I know are always looking for opportunities to refine their leadership skills. They never stop learning and expanding their practice. I've also written this book to honor them and stimulate their growth. It's my hope that the ideas the principals and mentors explore in this book will help readers with a wide range of experience grow their ability to lead their schools with increasing sophistication and effectiveness.

Outstanding leadership can't be reduced to easy recipes. The issues principals face are complex. They need more than abstract ideas or simple prescriptions. The dialogue format in this book provides opportunities to capture the everyday dilemmas, subtleties, and ambiguities that simple solutions miss … real people dealing with real problems.

What the Reader Can Expect

The dialogues begin with broad, foundational issues such as trust and focus and progress to the more specific topics such as hiring and growing teachers and running productive meetings.

Margaret Wheatley maintains that organizations, like nature, are stronger and more coherent when organized around a few simple ideas frequently repeated throughout the organization. Drawing on this idea, the reader will encounter a few powerful ideas and tools effectively applied to the variety of situations and problems principals face.

Special Features

Each chapter concludes with a section called "Becoming a Reflective Leader". Transformational principals are lead learners and thinkers in their schools. They tend to their own learning by journaling, reading, gathering the collective wisdom of their faculties, and engaging in focused conversations with mentors and colleagues.

At the end of each chapter, readers will find practical suggestions for incorporating these behaviors into their practice—behaviors that will deepen their thinking, develop their leadership skills, and provide the thought-provoking stimulation that fuels transformational leadership.

Conclusion

A principal's job often seems so busy there is no time to think. Great principals learn to reverse this equation. They spend as much time thinking as doing. Often their best thinking occurs during conversations with a mentor, coach, trusted friend, or a group of colleagues—thinking that is augmented by journaling, reading, and gathering the collective wisdom of their faculties.

Acknowledgments

Special thanks and deep gratitude to Susie Morice, my writing teacher, my editor-in-chief, and my inspiration. She has been a cheerleader, an intelligent critic, and a constant friend throughout the process of writing this book.

Thanks also to Kathy Kohm for encouraging me to keep going when I stumbled. She offered the insight and editorial know-how that allowed me to move forward.

Thanks to the teachers at Captain School and the principals I've mentored for their stories and dedication to improving their practice.

Thanks to my luncheon editorial crew for their insight and careful reading.

And a final thanks to Linda Henke from the Santa Fe Center for Educational Transformational Leadership for her constant inspiration, intellectual challenge, and encouragement.

1 Building Trust

Honesty and Clarity Are More Important Than Perfection

Outstanding principals build their success on a foundation of integrity. Teachers, parents, and students trust them because their words match their deeds; they honor commitments and say the same thing to all listeners. The trust they build enables them to successfully move through the inevitable rough patches of transforming schools.

Most principals *want* to match words with deeds and honor commitments. But because they're responsible to so many constituencies and face such complex problems, many find it difficult to be as clear and consistent as they'd like. As a result, other people assume selfish motives and perceive them as duplicitous. This lack of trust hampers their ability to lead their schools in positive directions.

In this chapter principals and their mentors discuss three ways to build trust in their communities:

- thinking out loud;
- separating intentions from actions and results;
- moving from an open door to an open school.

Thinking Out Loud

Principal: Kyle is the new principal of Oakville Middle School
Mentor: Catherine is a retired principal assigned to Kyle as a mentor

On a hot July day Kyle walked down the hall of Oakville Middle School, greeted the secretary, and exchanged a few words with the custodian. His heart pounded as he slid into the comfortable chair behind the large maple desk in his new office. He could hardly believe his luck. He had landed the job of middle school principal in one of the most innovative school districts in the area. He couldn't wait to introduce some ideas he'd been experimenting with at his old school where he'd been a science teacher and assistant principal.

During the summer Kyle held conferences with teachers and thought he had a good idea of the issues facing the school. At his old school, he'd initiated a conversation about grading practices and how they affected student achievement. This study led to changes in their grading system that contributed to increased student achievement. He was eager to begin a similar conversation at Oakville.

In August, Kyle received a call from his assigned mentor, Catherine Hill, a retired principal from a nearby district. He'd heard good things about her and the transformation she led at her old school. They set up a meeting in September. Catherine suggested Kyle buy a journal and record any observations, thoughts, and questions he'd like to discuss.

When Catherine arrived on a Monday in September, she noticed there was already student work up in the halls. School was in full swing. She checked in with the secretary and as she waited for Kyle, she noticed how efficiently and warmly the secretary dealt with parents and students who came in the office. Kyle ushered her into his office, asked her to sit down, and offered her coffee.

Catherine: I like what you've done with this office. I can see you're a reader. Me too. We'll have to exchange book titles. I'm also impressed with the student work I saw in the halls and the warmth and efficiency with which your secretary handled parents and students.

How has the first month been?

Kyle: Great! I get the feeling teachers really care about student learning and seem open to new ideas. There have been a lot of new initiatives in recent years. I think some teachers are scrambling to keep up. There have also been a number of changes in leadership. While everyone is welcoming, I suspect they are taking a wait-and-see attitude about me. I think I'll have to prove myself.

Catherine: Keen observations. What's next on your agenda?

Kyle: Teachers work hard to design effective learning activities. What's missing is a deeper look at how these activities are connected and ways structures such as grading might be affecting student achievement.

Catherine: How might you begin?

Kyle: The staff meets once a week after school for 45–60 minutes. Most of that time is spent on announcements and planning for future events. I'd like to change meetings to every other week for two hours. I'd reduce the number of announcements and make time for the faculty to learn together. I'd like to begin with discussions about the structures that affect students learning. We could start with how we grade student work.

Catherine: You've obviously given this a lot of thought, but I'm a little cautious. Grades are the foundation on which so much of traditional middle school education is based and you said some teachers are already feeling overwhelmed. I know you're eager to get started but you might want to go slowly. Why don't you start by journaling about some ways you might organize those discussions?

Kyle: Do you want me to write about anything specific?

Catherine: Just your ideas about how you would organize the meetings. It might be useful to read about dialogue in *The Adaptive School: A Sourcebook for Developing Collaborative Groups* by Robert Garmston and Bruce Wellman.[1]

When Kyle and Catherine met in late October fall was in the air and the school was abuzz with activity.

Catherine: What's happened since we last met?

Kyle: I've had a few parent complaints and discipline problems, but nothing major. As you suggested, I mapped out some possible staff agendas based on what I read about dialogue in *The Adaptive School*. The Oakville teachers have been working together as a team for a long time, so I'm not anticipating any problems.

Catherine: That sounds good, but before you get started, it might be useful to list any obstacles you think you might encounter.

Kyle: I don't know what you mean.

Catherine: It's always useful when launching a new initiative to slow down and think about potential obstacles, so you can avoid or prepare for them. This is particularly useful when you don't think there are obstacles. In my experience they're always are. It's just that you don't always see them. Some teachers might think these conversations are a waste of time, others might say they've been grading the same way for a long time with no complaints so why change.

Kyle: I see what you mean. I'll give it a shot. I'm hoping to start some preliminary conversations in November.

When they met in November, winter had begun and Kyle's honeymoon was over. Discipline referrals had increased, more parents were complaining, and many faculty conversations had become contentious. The faculty now seemed an obstacle rather than an engine of reform. Several teachers questioned Kyle's motives for initiating the conversations about grades; trust in his leadership was eroding. Teacher resistance was now at the head of the obstacles list Kyle made for Catherine.

Catherine: You look worried. What's going on?

Kyle: Our faculty discussions about grades have grown fractious. A few teachers seem interested, but most are questioning my motives for initiating these conversations. They think I have a hidden agenda. The math teachers assume I already have in mind the changes in grading I want to make and have organized the conversations to get them to buy in to decisions I've already made. When I say that's not true, they don't believe me. It's disheartening. I think of myself as a trustworthy guy.

Catherine: That's how I've experienced you. Explain again why you are organizing these conversations.

Kyle: Like you and I discussed, I want to begin an exploration of the strengths and weaknesses of our current grading system. I don't have anything specific in mind. I just want us to explore the assumptions on which we base our practice. The conventional wisdom is that grades motivate students to do better. I wonder if that's true. I want to see where our conversation leads us. We may or may not make any changes, but I hope we'll have a better understanding of the role grades play in our educational process when we're done. I want to use our time together to discover how our organizational structures affect student learning.

Catherine: Have you shared your thinking with the faculty?

Kyle: Not yet.

Catherine: Kyle, you have great ideas, you're a deep thinker, and you sincerely care about the education you offer students. It would be helpful if you shared those ideas and the thinking behind them with your faculty. Tell them what you just told me about exploring assumptions on which they base their practice. If you developed the habit of *thinking out loud*, you'd go a long way toward building the trust you need to move your school forward.

Kyle: I'm not sure I know what you mean.

Catherine: *Thinking out loud* is an important leadership skill. It means explaining the thinking behind your decisions. It means saying things like this:

- The reason I'd like to initiate these conversations is …
- The reason I made that decision is …
- I plan to make a decision later in the week, but first I'd like to hear everyone's thoughts.
- At this point, I'm considering several options, but I'm not yet ready to make a decision.
- The reason I'm questioning the wisdom of that idea is …
- I'm excited about that idea, but I'm also concerned that …
- I'm still undecided. I could be persuaded to go either way.

As you develop the habit of *thinking out loud*, you'll find that concern and suspicion about your motives will melt away. Others won't always agree with you, but since they know your thinking, they'll be able to engage in conversations with you that focus on your ideas rather than your personality or motivation. It will have the added benefit of forcing you to clarify your thinking.

When this happens, I predict teachers will begin to trust you, your reputation for integrity will rise, and you'll be able to create the strong, productive learning culture for Oakville students and teachers you envision. My own motto is *to say out loud as much truth as I can stand*. When I first started thinking out loud, it was scary. Some of my ideas were not yet fully developed and some turned out to be flat out wrong. But I found people to be very forgiving, particularly if I was clear and stayed open to their ideas. I found I made fewer mistakes and had less pushback when I shared my thinking with folks as we went along.

During the next month, record in your journal opportunities you have to *think out loud* and the effect thinking out loud has on other people and your own thinking.

Separating Intentions from Actions

Principal: Jessica is a third year principal at Jefferson Elementary School
Mentor: Brad is a veteran principal from another school in her district

Jessica had been principal of Jefferson Elementary for three years when the state department of education designated an adjacent school district as failing. As a result, students from the failing district could be bused to her district. This meant integrating students from an area that had been economically and academically impoverished into her predominately middle class school.

Jessica worked with teachers to make certain the new children and their families felt welcome and their social and academic needs were addressed. For the first month things went pretty well. However, around the middle of October the bus company began to report problems. There were four siblings on the bus: when one got involved in a fight, the others jumped in causing a major disturbance and an unsafe situation for everyone.

When Jessica called the students' mother, she said her children were doing exactly what she told them to do. She said her neighborhood was a dangerous place and she taught her children to defend one another. She thought it would be confusing if she suddenly told them to stop. Jessica was stuck. She didn't trust the mother's solution, and the mother didn't trust hers.

During her first two years as principal of Jefferson Elementary, Jessica had benefited from conversations with Brad, a veteran principal from another school in her district. She e-mailed Brad and set up a Skype session.

Jessica: Thanks, Brad, for taking time to talk to me. I have a bus problem. It started out small but has blown up into an issue I'm spending too much time on and getting nowhere. Even worse, I think I'm eroding rather than building trust with this family. They have four siblings that ride the bus together. The bus company called to report that squabbles or downright fights occur almost daily involving these students. The situation is unsafe for them and everyone else. I've tried exacting punishments but Mom always undermines me by insisting her kids are doing exactly what she's taught them to do—defend one another. This puts me in an adversarial position with her and erodes the trust I've worked so hard to build with the families who have transferred to our district.

Brad: I had a similar situation. It took me a long time and several rounds with the mother, but we finally solved the problem and perhaps most important I learned some important lessons that have helped me solve many problems since then. I learned to separate intentions from actions, to use intentions to find common ground, and to enlist the other person's help in solving the problem.

I read somewhere that we tend *to judge ourselves by our intentions and other people by their actions.* Looking at problems through that lens has been helpful to me in many situations, but it's been particularly useful when I'm in a conflict and trying to find common ground with an adversary. Typically, I find our intentions are the same or at least similar. Once we agree on our intentions or goals, it's easier to focus on actions that will help us achieve those goals. In your case, your intentions and the mother's are to transport her kids back and forth to school safely. What you disagree about is not the end but the means to that end.

Jessica: I'm sure you're right. How do I get agreement on the means?

Brad: I'd begin by framing the problem about intentions. "I think we both want the same thing—to safely transport your children to and from school." What might you say next?

Jessica: I could say something like, "I know you want to keep your children safe. I want that too. And I think the children want to follow your instructions. But these squabbles and fights are making the ride unsafe for them and the other children on the bus. If we work together, I think we can solve this problem. You know your children best. What can we do to help them stay safely in their seats and at the same time take care of one another?"

Brad: That sounds great. In my case, the mother and I agreed that if I got a referral from the bus company instead of solving the problem myself, I would call her and we would decide together what to do. She agreed to instruct the children to tell the bus driver if someone bothered them rather than trying to solve the problem by fighting. Things didn't immediately go smoothly. The first few times I called, we worked out consequences together. Since we were now partners instead of adversaries, it was easier for her to back me up. After a while, she said I didn't need to call her any more, I should just take care of the situation myself. Trust had been established. The bus incidents faded away.

Jessica: That's a great story. You've given me a lot to think about. Whenever we talk about one problem, what I learn seems to help me in a host of other situations. I'll try to practice *separating intentions from actions* in myself and with other people. I'll look for common ground and work to solve problems collaboratively. This may not be easy, and I suspect I'll need some support. Can we Skype again next month?

Brad: Absolutely! I'm learning as much as you are. I still need to continually remind myself to recognize intentions before reacting to actions. What if we each did some journaling about incidences that occur during the next month when we reacted (or failed to react) to intentions before we dealt with actions? We could discuss them when we Skype next month.

I just remembered a book I read a long time ago called *Getting to Yes: Negotiating Agreement Without Giving In.*[2] The authors, who had negotiated international treaties, told a simple story that illustrates the power of focusing on intentions or ultimate goals rather than actions. Two people were sitting in the library reading. One wanted the window open. The other wanted it closed. They tried leaving it halfway open (a compromise) but that left them both uncomfortable. As long as they focused on the window there seemed to be no mutually acceptable solution. However, a switch from actions (opening or closing the window) to their intentions (establishing a comfortable temperature in the room for everyone) opened up new possibilities. They opened the window in the next room so the wind wasn't blowing on anyone, and the temperature was right for both of them.

Jessica: That's just what you did with the mother and the bus problem.

Brad: Yep! That's where I learned it. I've used the idea so much it's now part of how I do business.

Jessica found that as she recognized people's intentions rather than simply reacting to their actions, their trust in her ability to lead grew. This, in turn, enabled her to solve problems more efficiently and effectively. She found she was no longer dealing with the same problems over and over again.

From an Open Door to an Open School

Principal: Shamele is the principal of a newly opened charter school
Mentor: Shawn is an old friend with many years of teaching experience

Shamele is a smart young African-American woman with a big mission. As a child she was bused from her urban neighborhood to a wealthy, predominately white, suburban school district where she reports she received an excellent education. Although pleased with her education, she was not happy she had to leave her neighborhood, and worries about students left behind in a failing district.

When she opened the doors of the City Learning Academy, she was prepared for many of the challenges she faced including moves to and from two temporary locations before settling into the school's permanent home. She was not prepared for the complaints she received from teachers and parents and the general level of discontent that always seemed to pervade the faculty.

This was particularly confusing and disheartening because Shamele had made a point of telling teachers and parents that her door was always open and had made a sincere effort to listen to people who came to talk. She was surprised how few people came, but they often said they were speaking for others so she assumed she was hearing what everyone thought.

Shamele was trying to meet everyone's needs. Yet, the harder she tried the less they seemed to trust her. She e-mailed Shawn, an old friend with many years of teaching experience, and asked if they could meet for coffee.

Shawn: I'm glad you e-mailed. I've been looking forward to seeing you. Tell me what's up?

Shamele: It's been hectic. Everything's harder than I thought it would be. Our fund-raising efforts are falling short for our new building and we're struggling to meet the state academic standards. Our financial issues are really just cash flow problems that will be resolved as we enroll more students. When we get our special education issues straightened out and when teachers feel more comfortable with the curriculum, our test scores will rise.

We can meet these challenges, but it will take a lot of work on everyone's part. This means teachers will need to devote all their time and energy to classroom instruction. Instead, they seem to be squabbling and complaining. Their energy and optimism are waning just when we need them the most.

Shawn: How do you know they're complaining?

Shamele: They come and tell me. I've told them my door is always open and I try to listen carefully to those who come to talk, but it doesn't stop the complaining.

Shawn: Think for a minute. How many teachers actually come to talk?

Shamele: It seems like a lot, but I guess it's only a few. But those few come often and tell me they're speaking for other people.

Shawn: I've worked in a number of schools. Each had its own particular culture which was strongly influenced by the way the principal managed the flow of information. The schools I most enjoyed and where I felt I did my best work were those where information was easily accessible to a wide range of people. Because everyone knew what was going on, there was no speculation about people's motives. The formation of in-groups and out-groups I'd experienced in other schools just didn't happen. Because we trusted one another, we were able to work together to build the structures, provide the support, and overcome obstacles to provide a first class education to all our students.

Surprisingly, in schools where some people were more in the know than others, principals often had an open door policy. Although these principals frequently said, "My door is always open," only a few people actually came to talk. Most faculty members learned about the principal's thinking through the filter of the few who took advantage of the open door. After a while, teachers began to see the people who talked directly to the principal as an in-group that had the principal's ear and relied on these people to tell them (the out-group) what was really going on or to voice their concerns. This indirect communication fostered gossip and speculation. People had a hard time developing a spirit of trust and collaboration.

In these schools there always seemed to be a *meeting after the meeting*. After staff meetings teachers gathered in small groups in the parking lot to say the things to like-minded colleagues they didn't feel comfortable saying during the official meeting. I noticed that after conferences with parents, teachers in these schools often met to express ideas they felt uncomfortable saying directly to parents. Not speaking directly and honestly eroded trust.

Shamele: So what's the answer? Having an open door policy sounds like such a good idea.

Shawn: The problem wasn't having an open door policy. It was not having enough other ways to disseminate information. The most effective schools were those where everyone's thinking was valued and expected and where the principal made a concerted effort to ensure multiple ways for people to get information directly rather than indirectly through gossip or speculation.

Shamele: It sounds like you're talking about *moving from an open door to an open school*. How can I get started?

Shawn: Start with a bit of action research about how information (formal and informal) currently flows in your school. Get teachers involved. Devote a staff meeting to this effort and/or send out a brief survey. The important thing is to include the whole faculty. Look at *The Adaptive School: A Sourcebook for Developing Collaborative Groups* by Robert Garmston and Bruce Wellman for ideas about how to organize meetings that allow everyone's participation in a timely manner.[1]

Start by changing your own behavior. Rather than having in-depth conversations with individual teachers about issues that potentially affect the entire school, suggest putting the issues on the next staff meeting agenda so everyone can participate in the conversation. Look for other ways to communicate information in direct and timely ways to the entire faculty. In-groups and out-groups will melt away, trust in your leadership and among faculty members will rise, and you'll find it easier to move your school forward.

Shamele: I'm going to need some help, particularly in organizing staff meetings in a way that allows every voice to be heard, but doesn't drag our meetings on forever. Could we meet once a month for the next few months?

Shawn: Sure. My current principal is good at building a collaborative culture by keeping information flowing. She has an open door policy, but more important, as you said, we have an open school and that makes all the difference. I'll pay closer attention to the things she does to accomplish this. Journal about your efforts. Start by paying attention to how information flows in your school now. How do the quiet people, who avoid your office, find out what's going on and how do the rest of you learn what they're thinking?

Shamele: I'm not a great journaler.

Shawn: Neither was I. But after I read *Educating the Reflective Practitioner* by Donald Schoen,[3] I became a journaler. He says principals, teachers, and students learn and grow when they engage in two important practices, *reflective journaling* that helps them know and clarify their thinking and *reflective conversation* that helps them deepen and refine their thinking. At first, I had trouble disciplining myself to journal. But once I got started, I found it so useful, I actually look forward to the few minutes I spend recording by thoughts, struggles, and accomplishments.

Shamele: I'll give it a try.

Shawn: Stick with it; write in your journal every day even if it's only for a few minutes for the first month to establish the habit. Schoen talks about three kinds of reflection: before, during, and after the event. I've found that useful in organizing my journal entries.

Shamele: I will. Thanks, Shawn.

Shawn: I think we'll learn a lot working together. Thanks for initiating these talks.

Conclusion

By thinking out loud, principals become clearer, deeper thinkers who invite the kind of feedback that helps them sharpen their perceptions and improve their communication. They build trust by eliminating speculation about their motives and find that other people trust honesty and clarity more than perfection. Separating intentions from actions and moving from an open door to an open school allow principals to build the trust they need to transform their schools into vital, growing institutions.

Strategies for Becoming a Reflective Leader

Transformational leaders are the lead learners in their schools. Their learning

- provides a model for teachers and students;
- enables them to work with teachers to learn through the difficulties that inevitably come with growth;
- deepens their personal understanding of the iterative nature of learning.

They tend to their learning by regularly

- journaling;
- having reflective conversations with mentors;
- reading;
- gathering the collective wisdom of their faculties;
- practicing new behaviors.

Thinking Out Loud

- Practice *thinking out loud* and notice the effect it has on other people, your ability to build trust, and clearly articulate your ideas.
- Record four such incidents in your journal.
- Bring these observations to your next mentoring session.

Separating Intentions From Actions

- Record four incidents when you affirmed or failed to affirm intentions before you dealt with actions. Divide a page into four columns. In the first column, record the incident; in the second, your reaction; and in the third, a possible alternative reaction. In the fourth column, explore the possible result to each of your actions.
- Discuss journal entries with your mentor.
- Practice affirming intentions before dealing with behavior.

From an Open Door to an Open School

- Keep track of who is coming (and not coming) to your office and which issues get talked about in the privacy of your office and which in public meetings.
- Don't let one person speak for or about other people.
- Ask folks who come to talk to you about school issues to put them on the agenda for the next staff meeting or include them in the weekly memo.
- Move as much communication as possible to public forums in order to keep everyone in the know and avoid in-groups and out-groups.

Citations

1. Robert Garmston and Bruce Wellman, *The Adaptive School: A Sourcebook for Developing Collaborative Groups* (Lanham, MD: Roman and Littlefield, 2016).
2. Roger Fisher, William Ury, and Bruce Patton, *Getting to Yes: Negotiating Agreement Without Giving In* (New York, NY: Penguin Books, 1991).
3. Donald Schoen, *Educating the Reflective Practitioner* (New York, NY: Jossey-Bass Inc., 1983).

Additional Reading

Charles Feltman, *The Thin Book of Trust: An Essential Primer for Building Trust at Work* (Bend, OR: Thin Book Publishing, 2009).

2 Establishing and Maintaining Focus

Knowing What Not to Do Is as Important as Knowing What to Do

A myriad of legitimate issues constantly compete for a principal's time and energy. Ordinary principals work hard to meet these demands and often feel overwhelmed. Because their goals are vague and their commitment to them is weak, it's difficult to say no to competing demands. As a result, their efforts are diffused over a broad range of objectives and although they and their teachers work hard, they achieve only moderate results. Their schools may have great teachers but they never become great schools because they lack the synergy that results from a clear common focus that allows everyone to pull in the same direction.

When all teachers are moving in the same direction, they reinforce one another's efforts. As a result, they accomplish things individual teachers could never accomplish alone. This creates optimism and efficacy that is lacking when efforts are fragmented and every activity has equal weight. Great principals help teachers focus their time and energy on mutually agreed on values and goals. They understand that deciding what not to do is often as important as what to do.

In this chapter, principals and their mentors discuss the following ways to develop and maintain a clear, consistent focus. They work with teachers to collectively answer the questions:

- How do we want to work together? (core values)
- Where do we want to go? (clear, consistent, common focus)
- How are we going to get there? (annual goals)

They reference the answers to these questions when decisions are made. As a result, they become sign posts that give direction and meaning to all teaching and learning activities.

Establishing a Clear, Consistent, Common Focus

Principal: Kyle is the new principal of Oakville Middle School
Mentor: Catherine is a retired principal assigned to Kyle as a mentor

Kyle: Thinking out loud has made such a difference in my life. It has improved my relationship with my family and the people in the central office, as well as everyone at Oakville Middle School. My wife said to be sure and thank you. She says she understands me better, and I've been easier to live with since I started thinking out loud.

Catherine: I'm not surprised. You're a thoughtful person. Letting folks know what you're thinking keeps conversations focused on your ideas, not others' guesses about your thinking.

Kyle: You used the word focus. That's the next thing I'd like to talk about. Teachers are working like crazy, but it feels like we're spinning our wheels. There are a million demands on everyone's time and energy. Almost all these demands represent some good we might do. But we can't do them all. It feels like we're running as fast as we can and getting farther behind. I'm afraid the good will we have now may turn to cynicism if this continues.

Catherine: I know it's difficult when teachers are working hard, but the school is not achieving positive results. It's often because everyone is pulling in a different direction. What have you done to establish a common focus?

Kyle: At our last staff meeting, I tried to initiate a conversation about writing a mission statement and establishing some annual goals. The teachers said their mission has been "to do what's best for kids" and their annual goals (which are set at the district level) were to improve their test scores in math and language arts. They said teachers did what they thought their students needed, what parents said they wanted, and what federal and state law required. This seems too vague and individualistic.

I've found little evidence of any common commitments to help focus the faculty's everyday decisions about where to spend their time and energy. They've never had conversations about their beliefs and never worked together to develop core values they agree to honor. Their mission and goals seem to be lifeless statements with little relevance to their everyday work.

The thing teachers seem to value most is their autonomy. They said my predecessor trusted them to do the right thing. They valued the confidence he placed in them. As a result, they seem reluctant to write more specific goals. I don't blame them. Although I'd like to move beyond their reluctance, I can understand why it's there. At my old school, every year we went through the process of writing a mission statement and setting goals. The principal posted them on the wall in the teachers' workroom, printed them on staff meeting agendas, and sent them to central office. They had little bearing on the actual work we did. Everyone considered them a massive waste of time.

Catherine: I've worked in schools where the same thing happened. The problem was either that teachers didn't have a significant role in establishing them or the principal failed to help teachers use the mission and goals as guideposts for making decisions. As a result, they *were* a waste of time and, even worse, empty promises.

That vague sense of collective focus might have worked before we committed ourselves to developing a high level of competence in *all* our students. We can no longer afford to waste the most precious resources we have, our time and energy, by defusing them over a wide range of disparate goals.

When I hear about a school without a clear, collective focus, I'm reminded of a team of horses hitched to one another but pulling in different directions. Although many may be strong, their lack of a common focus inhibits their individual and collective effectiveness. When they all pull in the same direction they enhance rather than inhibit one another's efforts.

Developing a clear sense of mission and setting mutually agreed-on goals points everyone in the same direction and establishing core values keeps them running at top speed. Instead of diminishing, their capacity actually multiplies, and they begin to accomplish things no one could do alone.

Kyle: If we don't make some changes, I think we're heading for a massive burnout.

Catherine: I had a similar situation. When I arrived at my last school, teachers were operating as "independent contractors." Everyone did his/her own thing. As a result, teaching was uneven. Because many of our students came from middle and upper middle class homes and we measured our effectiveness by average test scores, we looked okay. However, when we received a number of new students as part of a racial desegregation plan, began to disaggregate our scores, and paid attention to our data, we realized this lack of consistency wasn't good for anyone and it was harmful for many students, particularly the most vulnerable.

Students who entered kindergarten behind their classmates never caught up. In fact, they fell farther behind. I was reading about new ways to teach reading and writing. That summer I attended the Harvard Principals' Academy where I heard testimonies from principals who had implemented these new ideas. I thought they might help us do a better job of reaching all our students.

My excitement was shared by many teachers who also had been reading about and experimenting with these new ideas and were eager to fully implement them in their classrooms. I was so focused on the teachers who shared my excitement, I failed to notice the teachers and parents who weren't interested in changing. This created confusion and anger among teachers and parents. I'd inadvertently created a crisis. I needed a crash course in leadership.

Kyle: I can't imagine. You're so well thought of in the community.

Catherine: That's because I'm talking to you in retrospect. In the middle, our change process seemed like one big mess. What I'm going to describe didn't happen all at once. It took years. We were constantly trying to learn from our mistakes and continually refining our work. *Change is never as tidy as it's presented after the fact. The important thing is that we kept moving forward, kept learning, and kept refining our practice.* You'll have to develop your own process, but I'm hoping our journey will give you some things to think about.

Kyle: You've already helped by acknowledging the confusion change causes. It always seems so tidy when you read about it.

Catherine: I realized early on a few important things. First, the whole faculty would have to work together *to learn and plan our way forward.*

We needed everyone's thinking. A plan developed by a few people who asked others to buy in to their ideas would not work. Second, we needed a way to think about and communicate to others what at the time seemed like a messy and confusing process. I began to tell people our change process was like my front lawn.

Kyle: What's with the metaphors ... a team of horses and your front lawn?

Catherine: Having a picture in mind helps me understand and communicate what's happening in complex situations like school change. Metaphors are an important leadership tool. When used appropriately, they become a visual shorthand for describing complexity.

Kyle: What about your front lawn?

Catherine: I planted Zoysia grass last spring. I put plugs in the ground in a random order. I didn't plant them all at once. Whenever I had some time I added a few more plugs. At first, it looked like nothing was happening, but if you looked closely little shoots were beginning to appear that connected one plug with another. I kept watering and adding plugs as needed and eventually the plugs were all connected to create a beautiful lawn. That's what we did at Oxford Elementary. We'd identify a need and put in a plug. Eventually the plugs began to connect with one another and we had a strong system where all sectors were connected and each sector nourished the others. Just as the thick grass crowded out the weeds, our system crowded out efforts not central to our focus. Although our process wasn't linear, all our efforts were connected.

Kyle: You didn't have the change process all planned before you began?

Where Do We Want to Go? (Clear, Consistent, Common Focus)

Catherine: No. We began by asking ourselves where we wanted to go ... the first plug in our lawn. We used a regularly scheduled staff meeting to brainstorm ideas, then we used *dot voting* to establish priorities. (We gave participants two sticky dots and ask them to place the dots next to the ideas they thought most important.) This created a quick, clear visual of the group's priorities. I took the notes from this meeting and fashioned a mission statement. I presented it to the staff for additions, corrections, and approval at the next staff meeting. The top priorities were: 1) to enable all our students to demonstrate high levels of proficiency and 2) to take responsibility for achieving this goal ourselves.

There were important commitments in these ideas. Commitments that changed the way we did business. First, we said we were committed to educating *all* our students at high levels of proficiency, not just those we thought were the brightest or the most cooperative. Although high levels of proficiency was rather vague and needed further definition, it meant we could no longer put children in low ability groups and lower what we expected of them. We said we'd take responsibility for their achievement. This meant we could no longer blame their parents, the central office, or the children themselves for their poor progress. We decided that although many of the things that hampered students' learning were not our fault, their learning at school was our responsibility.

We had agreed on some important ideas. Ideas that became the mission statement that provided a mutually agreed on focus and dramatically changed our culture. My job was to help teachers translate these ideas into everyday reality.

Kyle: I have a friend who's a principal. His district's mission is "To inspire and prepare students as leaders, scholars, stewards, and citizens for a diverse and changing world." This focus is apparent in all their schools. Curriculum, instruction, and even discipline plans are all based on this statement. Students are recommended for commendation in each of these categories.

Catherine: In *Taking Charge: Leading with Passion and Purpose in the Principalship*, Paul Shaw says the mission statement at his school is "To improve the life chances of every student."[2] When plans are made, the faculty continually asks how a particular plan or decision improves the life chances of their students. I'm currently on a planning committee for a group that hopes to open a new charter school in a low-income city neighborhood. They borrowed Paul Shaw's idea and added their own twist: "To develop the competencies and habits of mind that will improve the life chances of every student."

Another friend works at a school whose mission statement is to develop students as competent and confident learners.

All these statements have three important characteristics:

- They were developed by teachers, not imposed by others.
- They guide everyday decisions about curriculum, instruction, and discipline.
- They are reviewed periodically.

Kyle: I'll keep those examples in mind and check out Shaw's book, but right now I'd like to get back to you and what you did at your school. Your results were good, but you describe your process as chaotic. If you had it to do again, would you use the same process?

Catherine: I don't think so. I've learned a lot since then. After I read about "The Focusing Four" (Figure 2.1), a more structured way to brainstorm and set priorities, in *The Adaptive School,*[1] we used this strategy to set annual goals and develop core values. We also added more information and more people to the process.

Brainstorm

- Record brainstormed ideas on chart paper
- Elicit ideas only
- Discourage criticism or questions
- Push for between 8–18 ideas

Clarify

- Ask if any items need to be clarified
- The author provides the clarification
- Facilitator observes the questioner during clarification and stops the clarification when questioner indicates nonverbally or otherwise that he/she understands

Advocate

- Participants may advocate for as many items as they wish and as many times as they wish
- Statements of advocacy must be phrased in the positive
- Statements of advocacy must be brief

Canvass

- Ask individuals in the group to identify which few of the ideas they feel are most important
- To determine what a few is, use the formula: one-third plus one (If there are 12 items on the list, ask the group to identify 5 which are most important to them; if there are 15 items on the list, ask the group to identify 6). They do not need to be placed in rank order.
- Take a hand count to determine which items are of greatest interest to the group

Figure 2.1 The Focusing Four

Source: Adapted from: R. Garmston and B. Wellman, *The adaptive school: Developing and facilitating collaborative groups syllabus* (Norwood, MA: Christopher-Gordon Publishers, 2000, p. 90).

Kyle: I have that book on my shelf.

Catherine: Our mission statement proved helpful in keeping us focused as we worked through the difficulties of developing and implementing a new curriculum and a different instructional approach. But it wasn't enough. Now that we were using our staff meetings to discuss real issues that mattered to all of us, we needed guidelines for how we would work together. We were moving from independent contractors to a cohesive group and we needed to sharpen our collaboration skills.

Kyle: What did you do?

How Do We Want to Work Together? (Core Values)

Catherine: We put in another plug. We used "The Focusing Four" to answer the question, "How do we want to work together?" We called our answers core values. Values that along with the commitments we made in our mission statement dramatically changed our culture. Margaret Wheatley's *Leadership and the New Science* discusses complex systems in nature that are organized around a few simple principles rather than complicated top-down directives.[3]

These were our organizing principles:

- **Assume good will**. We constantly reminded each other and ourselves about this. It didn't come easily. We had to give up feeling self-righteous and look at situations from someone else's perspective.
- **Bring issues to the table**. This also required monitoring. It was often easier to talk only to like-minded colleagues privately than to confront issues directly during staff meetings.
- **Focus on learning**. Our students and our own learning became the focus of everything we did. When the benefits were not worth the expenditure of time, effort, and/or money, some sacred traditions had to go.
- **Involve all people affected by a decision in the decision-making process.** We invited students to parent conferences, parents to student staffings, and teachers to plan the allocation of resources. Thinking and planning with others forced us to be more honest with our colleagues and ourselves.

How Are We Going to Get There? (Annual Goals)

Catherine: We now had two plugs in our lawn. Our mission statement told us what we wanted to accomplish. Our core values set standards for how we would work together. Now we needed to establish a map for how to reach our destination. We needed annual goals.

Kyle: I may run into some pushback here. The district already sets annual goals, and we're already loaded with meetings. One more might be one too many. Maybe I should start with our leadership team.

Catherine: Our experience was different. Some teachers were reluctant at first, but when they realized they had a real voice in making decisions about things that directly affected their work with students, they were mostly eager to participate.

I'm cautious about leadership teams. I'm always worried about creating "in-groups" and "out-groups." Out-groups often become silent and rob their schools of their thinking or are oppositional and slow the progress of new initiatives. In-groups become exclusive and over-protective of the status quo. As long as, over time, a wide range of staff members serve on the team and there are many opportunities for the rest of the staff to participate in important decisions, I think they're okay; although, in small schools I think they're unnecessary.

Kyle: I've always worked in schools with leadership teams. I never gave it much thought.

Catherine: The lesson here that's more important than leadership teams is to question all the systems, structures, and traditions in your school to see if they are moving you in the direction you want to go or if they've outlived their usefulness.

Kyle: That's a big assignment. I know there are always people who are attached to certain traditions and don't want them changed.

Catherine: Just suggesting you keep your eyes open. Continually ask yourself and your faculty which traditions and systems have outlived their usefulness and which are the glue that holds a community together. It can be a difficult call but it's the art of leadership.

At Oxford Elementary we didn't have a leadership team so I asked for volunteers who were interested in helping to plan a goal-setting meeting. Six volunteers met after school. We decided to use "The Focusing Four" to organize the meeting and to put together a packet of material (standardized test scores, discipline referrals, district mission statements and goals) to distribute to the staff a week before the meeting to create a context for our deliberations. (Two more plugs.)

After the first few years, parents asked if they could be part of the goal-setting process. The answer, of course, was "yes." We were slightly embarrassed we hadn't thought of this ourselves. We needed their voices. But we wanted a full range of parent voices, not just the PTO officers or the active parents who had the time and inclination to participate at school. I met with a PTO committee who organized an evening meeting for all Oxford parents. They divided the parents who attended the meeting into groups of eight. Each group brainstormed the answer to two questions:

- What makes Oxford a great school?
- What would make it even better?

They recorded their answers on chart paper and posted the sheets on the walls of the staff meeting room where the faculty met to develop annual goals. The Committee used our weekly parent newsletter to ask the same questions of those parents who couldn't attend the evening meeting—another plug.

Kyle: I imagine that by giving parents a legitimate role in the planning process, you curtail the parent complaints that use so much time.

Catherine: Exactly! In addition, we got the benefit of their thinking upfront while we were still in the planning process rather than complaining after the fact. Another plug in the lawn and the horses were beginning to pull as a team. The various groups that made up our school community were focused on the same goals and objectives.

Kyle: Returning to those metaphors.

Catherine: Another leadership lesson: the metaphors, quotes, and stories you tell bind your community together and keep them focused. Even if folks tease you about them (or maybe particularly if they do) they are important leadership tools. One of your central jobs as a leader is to inspire teachers, students, and parents to think big, be creative, and do their best work. Metaphors, quotes, and stories are important tools in this endeavor. You're the keeper of your school's on-going narrative. Make certain you intentionally craft that narrative in the direction you want it to go.

Speaking of metaphors, I saw *Les Misérables* last night. Victor Hugo used the metaphor of a rope to illustrate the power of focused group effort. A rope is made up of many different strands each of which is individually weak, but when woven together becomes very strong.

Kyle: I'm going to borrow your metaphors.

Catherine: Good! Eventually, we began to prepare for our annual goal-setting meeting with a series of meetings that focused on the allocation of resources. We decided our district had given us four resources to accomplish our mission (time, space, money, personnel). We wanted to ensure these resources were aligned with our goals.

We invited any interested staff member to attend a series of meetings, each focused on the allocation of one of these resources. The Time Committee developed the schedule; the Space Committee the plan for the location of various classes and activities; the Money Committee the budget; and the Personnel Committee a process for interviewing teacher candidates. Each committee wrote a plan focusing resources on our mission and goals. For example, one of our academic goals was to allow large blocks of uninterrupted time for literacy instruction. This had implications for the Time Committee. One year we decided to build up our library, and another year we decided to increase technology. These had implications for the Money Committee. Focusing involved organizing our resources as well as ourselves to achieve our goals. The committees presented the plans they developed to the faculty as a whole for approval and inclusion in our annual goals. No one was required to attend any of these meetings, but they were well attended because we were making decisions important to everyone's work.

Finally armed with the reports and background information, we met in late May to establish our goals for the following school year. We reviewed the information we'd gathered and once again used "The Focusing Four" and "Dot Voting" to set priorities.

Great principals understand that unless stakeholders have a role in developing goals, they don't have the energy and commitment it takes to reach them. As a result, the principal's role shifts from the person who sets the goals to the person who establishes the structures that allow others to establish their goals.

Kyle: That's not any easy shift. You'd have to give up some control or maybe a lot of control. How do you keep things from getting out of control?

Catherine: It's not for the faint of heart. At first, it seemed scary. I was concerned about the control issue and I was afraid people would see me as indecisive. Instead, the opposite happened. The staff began to control itself and as teachers assumed more responsibility for the school as a whole, we all became stronger and more in control. Instead of subtly sabotaging our efforts, the whole staff felt responsible for ensuring their success. If you decide to move in this direction, we'll have many opportunities to discuss the details.

Kyle: I hope so.

Catherine: Our goal-setting meeting usually took 3 or 4 hours. We ordered pizza and organized ourselves so every voice could be heard—more about that in a future conversation. (See Chapter 8, Planning Meetings.) I took the results of our deliberations, did a little wordsmithing, and e-mailed the results to the staff. When we met again in August to plan the next school year, we hammered out the details that enabled us to meet our goals—another plug.

As we started the next school year, our mission statement kept us facing toward the same destination. Our core values told us how to behave as we traveled together. And our annual goals provided a road map for how we would get there. We were so much stronger pulling in the same direction. Everyone held themselves and everyone else responsible for attaining our goals. Our horses were lined up, our lawn was lush, and our ropes were strong.

Kyle: WOW! I can't wait to get started. But I've learned to slow down a little and plan before I begin. Do you have any readings to suggest?

Catherine: I'd start with *Daring Greatly* by Brené Brown.[5] I was also greatly influenced by the work of Peter Senge, Margaret Wheatley, Robert Garmston, and Richard Dufour. Jot down any questions you have as you think about creating a productive focus for your own time and energy and the time, energy, and efforts of your faculty.

Conclusion

Beneath the surface of great schools lies a strong sense of mission and a process for developing, refining, and applying values and goals. Because there is a common focus, a synergy develops enhancing each person's individual efforts, and the same amount of time and energy yields better results. Because efforts are less fragmented and more productive, principals and teachers develop a spirit of energy and optimism that pervades their schools.

Strategies for Becoming a Reflective Leader

Gathering Collective Wisdom

Work with mentor, leadership team, or an ad hoc planning committee to set up meetings and develop agendas that enable teachers to collectively answer three questions:

- How do we want to work together? (core values)
- Where do we want to go? (mission statement)
- How are we going to get there? (annual goals)

Use the following references in planning these meetings:

- *The Adaptive School: A Sourcebook for Developing Collaborative Groups* by Robert Garmston and Bruce Wellman.[1]
- *Principals Who Learn: Asking the Right Questions, Seeking the Best Solutions* by Barbara Kohm and Beverly Nance.[4]

Hold three all-staff meetings (using the agendas developed by the planning committee) for teachers to develop:

- Core values. Gather core values from other schools. Ask teachers to add their ideas. Use dot voting to select three or four.
- Mission statement. Avoid platitudes and generalizations. Gather information on teachers' beliefs about teaching and learning as well as knowledge and habits of mind you want students to have when they graduate.
- Annual goals. Gather background material (district mission statement and goals, test scores, discipline records, etc.). Distribute these materials to teachers before the meeting. Write three or four actionable goals for

the next school year that respond to current needs and move you closer to the promise of your mission statement.

Reference the core values, mission statement, and annual goals when making decisions so they become signposts that give direction and meaning to all teaching and learning activities.

Journaling

Record five incidents you observe that illustrate activities that are (or are not) consistent with your core values, mission statement, and annual goals you develop with teachers.

Storytelling

- Tell stories about these incidents at staff meetings, in your weekly memo, or while chatting with teachers in the lunchroom.
- Provide a forum for teachers to tell their stories. A good place for this is the opening five minutes of staff meetings.

Citations

1. Robert Garmston and Bruce Wellman, *The Adaptive School: A Sourcebook for Developing Collaborative Groups* (Lanham, MD: Roman and Littlefield, 2016).
2. Paul Shaw, *Taking Charge: Leading With Passion and Purpose in the Principalship* (New York, NY: Teachers College Press, 2012).
3. Margaret Wheatley, *Leadership and the New Science: Learning About Organization from an Orderly Universe* (San Francisco, CA: Berrett-Koehler, 1992).
4. Barbara Kohm and Beverly Nance, *Principals Who Learn: Asking the Right Questions Seeking the Best Solutions* (Alexandria, VA: Association for Supervision and Curriculum Development, 2007).

5. Brené Brown, *Daring Greatly: How the Courage to Be Vulnerable Transforms the Way We Live, Love, Parent, and Lead* (New York, NY: Avery, 2015).

Additional Reading

Elena Aguilar, *The Art of Coaching: Effective Strategies for School Transformation* (San Francisco, CA: Jossey-Bass, 2013).

Linda Lambert, *Leadership Capacity for Lasting School Improvement* (Alexandria, VA: Association for Supervision and Curriculum Development, 2003).

3 Developing a Learning Culture

From Fixing People to Building Capacity

When schools are in trouble, it's easy to blame teachers and try to fix them. No one likes to be blamed or fixed, and quick fixes rarely work. Building teachers' capacity for learning and teaching is a more effective way to improve schools. Fixing teachers involves doing something *to* them. Building capacity involves doing something *with* them. The first creates pushback and results in superficial and temporary improvement. The second creates a positive momentum that feeds on itself and results in substantial, long-lasting, and continual growth.

In this chapter principals and their mentors discuss ways to build teachers' capacity for learning and teaching by:

- affirming past and current efforts;
- examining beliefs and connecting them to current pedagogical practice;
- organizing conversations about learning and teaching;
- working with teachers one-on-one;
- observing classroom practice.

Building Learning Capacity

Principal: Jessica is a third year principal at Jefferson Elementary School
Mentor: Brad is a veteran principal from another school in her district

Jessica's elementary school recently experienced a large influx of students from a nearby failing district. Despite teachers' efforts, test scores are falling and discipline problems rising.

Everyone is scrambling to find a fix. If students worked harder, parents were more supportive, teachers understood the curriculum better, everything would be okay. Students feel singled out, parents feel blamed, and teachers feel unsuccessful. Jessica called Brad and asked for a Skype session.

Jessica: Hi Brad. Can I pick your brain?

Brad: Sure What's up?

Jessica: When we spoke last month the problems we had with the influx of new students from Appleton seemed small and isolated, like the bus incident you helped me solve. Now they seem pervasive and difficult.

Brad: Like what?

Jessica: We used take pride in our test scores and gave ourselves credit for being great teachers. Since the Appleton students arrived, our test scores have fallen and everyone's looking for someone to blame. Teachers are the first target and a host of well-meaning folks (from the central office to the federal government) are scrambling to fix us. Teachers feel overloaded, unsuccessful, and resentful. The mood around here has gone from optimistic to angry and defensive.

Brad: I've learned that in the middle of a mess there are always learning opportunities. You and your teachers need to find those opportunities and learn your way forward.

Jessica: What does that mean?

Brad: What worked before is no longer sufficient. Blaming someone else or clinging to old ways won't work. They'll make things worse. Quick fixes won't work either. They'll cause pushback and get in the way of actually solving the problem. Instead you have to work with your faculty to increase their capacity for learning and teaching.

Jessica: If that involves asking them to do one more thing, I'm afraid I'm going to get a lot of pushback. Everyone's already exhausted and discouraged.

Brad: It probably does involve doing some different things, but if you work with teachers to help them increase their learning and teaching capacity rather than giving them a quick fix, you'll get appreciation rather than pushback ... at least eventually.

Jessica: I'm not sure I understand the difference between fixing teachers and increasing their capacity.

Affirm Past and Current Efforts

Brad: It seems like a contradiction, but *in order to help people grow you first have to accept and affirm them exactly as they currently are*. This enables them to open up to new learning. Without that affirmation, it feels like you think there's something wrong with them. Something you're trying to fix and they're trying to hide. This diminishes their capacity for learning and creates the backlash you're experiencing. It's the reason fixes rarely work.

As we began to make changes, a veteran teacher asked me, "Are you saying everything I've been doing for the past 20 years is wrong?" I replied, "Of course not, we're standing on your shoulders. As circumstances change, we need to change and we need to always be growing and getting better. *Learning is not a criticism of the past, it's a continual process of growth.*"

Examine Beliefs and Connect Them to Current Pedagogical Practice

Jessica: How do we start that process?

Brad: Help teachers think more deeply about their work … ask basic questions and question long-held assumptions.

Jessica: How?

Brad: Provide opportunities for teachers to think together about the foundations of their practice. I'd begin by helping them examine their beliefs about learning. Whether these beliefs are explicit or hidden, they have a strong influence on the way teachers teach. Such a discussion will open a path to deeper thinking about their practice. Let's talk about activities to help them articulate and share their beliefs.

Jessica: I recently read *Mindset* by Carol Dweck.[1] It might help if we all read at least the first chapter before the meeting. She distinguishes between a "growth mindset" and a "fixed mindset." I think most Jefferson teachers would say they believe in a "growth mindset" but I'm not sure we actually teach students that growth is possible and that risk and effort can make them smarter. We may unintentionally be telling many of them they're not smart enough and nothing they do can change that. Maybe we should talk about the book first and then explore our beliefs about learning.

Brad: It might be interesting and productive to help teachers examine the mindset they grew up with and how that influences their teaching today.

Jessica: Sounds like a lot for one meeting.

Brad: How often do you meet with your staff? How long are your meetings?

Jessica: We meet every other Monday for about and hour and 15 minutes.

Organize Opportunities for Teachers to Talk About Teaching and Learning

Brad: That's not long. I suggest you devote a meeting or two to examining your beliefs about teaching and learning and exploring whether your current practices are consistent with these beliefs. Then use a staff development day to make plans for the future based on what you learn.

Jessica: How would that look?

Brad: You know your teachers and the culture at your school better than I. How might you organize the first meeting?

Jessica: I'd ask them to read the first two chapters of *Mindset* before the meeting. I'd have them break into small groups to talk about their reactions to the book, which mindset prevailed in their homes and schools as they were growing up, and which mindset they think is prevalent at Jefferson.

Brad: That sounds like a great way to get started. Anything else?

Jessica: Next I'd have them brainstorm their beliefs about learning and teaching.

Brad: I assume they would still be in small groups. I think you might want a whole group activity to conclude the meeting. What about each small group presenting its brainstorm list to the whole group and dot voting to decide on the top five. You can use those five at the next meeting to explore ways you are currently teaching (or not teaching) those attitudes about learning to Jefferson students. Are you familiar with dot voting?

Jessica: You give each person several sticky dots and ask them to post them next to the items they think are most important. In a matter of minutes you have a visual representation of the group's priorities.

Brad: You have material for your first meeting. If you want to e-mail me your agenda, I'll look it over and give you feedback. Then let's set up a Skype session to plan the next meeting.

Jessica: You're on. Thanks so much.

Jessica's E-Mail

Agenda

3:45–4:00: Announcements

4:00–4:30: Small group discussions of *Mindset*, teachers' experiences growing up, and beliefs about learning they hold now. Record these lists on chart paper. (10 minutes on each topic.)

4:30–4:50: Quick reports to the whole group

4:50–5:00: Dot vote

Brad's E-Mail

This looks great. I like that you used a timed agenda. I think teachers will have a lot to think about after this meeting. I'd make up the small groups ahead of time and ask teachers to sit at tables with these groups as they walk in the meeting. This saves time and allows for a good mix of teachers at each table. I'd mix teachers from different grade levels and different disciplines, as well as different personalities and years of experience.

Jessica: Hi Brad, the meeting went well. The timing was tight, but I think teachers appreciated my efforts to respect their time. Following is the list of beliefs we brainstormed and dot voted on.

- Mistakes are opportunities to learn.
- Ability is not fixed; it can be grown.
- Descriptive rather than judgmental language promotes learning.

- Learning often requires repetition or successive approximations toward mastery.
- Learning requires a balance of safety and challenge. Too much safety, students exert little effort and little learning takes place. Too much challenge, students become overwhelmed and shut down.

Brad: A great list. What are your plans now?

Jessica: At our next staff meeting, I thought we'd divide our chart paper in three sections. In one column we'd put the beliefs we selected about learning. In the second, the ways we currently teach these attitudes, and in the third areas where we might improve.

For instance, in column 1 "We see mistakes as opportunities to learn." In column 2 "We talk about mistakes (our own and others) not a failures but as learning opportunities." And in column 3 "We often fail to give students opportunities to correct mistakes."

We can use our winter professional development day to create another column, "ways to incorporate these ideas into our everyday practice."

Brad: That reminds me. It's important to begin and end meetings exactly on time. It's a matter of respect and trust. It's why a timed agenda is important.

Jessica: A friend taught me that long ago. I started on time even if only a few people were present. As a result, everyone now comes on time. It's harder to end on time ... Sometimes I have to skip items or postpone them until the next meeting. I try to develop a more realistic agenda next time.

Brad: The way you organized these meetings will help teachers think more deeply about student learning and open them to new ideas.

In Peter Senge's book *Presence: Human Purpose and the Field of the Future* he says, "When people in leadership positions begin to serve a vision infused with a larger purpose, their work shifts naturally from producing results to encouraging the growth of people who produce the results."[2] Not a bad motto for principals. I'd call *Presence* recommended reading.

Jessica: So you're saying, if I help teachers reconnect to the larger purpose of education and think more deeply about their practice, they'll expand their capacity for learning and teaching and the whole school will grow.

Brad: Exactly. Students need teachers who are learning and growing themselves—teachers whose capacity for learning and skill in teaching is always expanding.

Working With Teachers One-on-One

Jessica: That sounds great, but we may also need some of the strategies embedded in those quick fixes. And I understand how powerful a group of teachers learning together can be, but I'm charged with evaluating teachers one by one, not in a group.

According to state law and our district's evaluation policy, I must observe non-tenured teachers and veteran teachers who are on the evaluation cycle at least three times and write a summary of my evaluations. I spend a lot of time doing this, but I feel as if my efforts don't necessarily translate into improved classroom practice.

Brad: I've experimented with ways to help me better understand what's going on in classrooms. In addition to my observations, I ask every teacher to schedule a conference with me some time during the school year and bring one of the following artifacts:

- a case study of a student who's struggling;
- samples of student work;
- a unit of study; or
- standardized test scores.

These artifacts help ground our conversations in the concrete realities of classroom learning. My goal is to help teachers grow and me understand their thinking. I'm getting better at asking the kind of basic questions that promote growth.

Jessica: Like what?

Brad: Really basic stuff like:

- Why did you decide to remove Johnny from the group?
- Why did you pick this strategy?
- Why have you organized the lesson this way? Was it effective? How do you know? How might you vary it in the future?
- I'm wondering why Jessie was so confused about fractions.
- How do you know when everyone has mastered this concept?

- What happens if everyone but two or three students has mastered a concept?
- What's the next thing you need to learn to improve your practice in this area?
- What have you learned from these test scores that will improve student learning?

Jessica: I can see how powerful such conversations could be. Especially if we can get beyond them just trying to impress me and really explore the deeper issues involved in teaching and learning. But it sounds time consuming.

Brad: It is. I reserve one morning a week all year for these talks. That's how important I think they are. In a book I recently read called *From Systems Thinking to Systemic Action* by Lee Jenkins he says an outstanding administrator is "A person who believes the very best use of his time is providing learning and growth opportunities for others."[3] Structuring staff meetings to explore beliefs about learning and talks with teachers about their work serves this goal.

Notice how you're spending your time. If a good chunk of it isn't devoted to building teachers' capacity to meet student needs, it's time to reassess.

Improving Instruction: Learning Together

Principal: Shamele is the principal of a newly opened charter school
Mentor: Shawn is an old friend with many years of teaching experience

Test scores at Shamele's school are falling and the representative from the state department of education is threatening to shut her down. Shamele turns to her friend Shawn.

Shamele: I need help. Our kids are smart and our teachers are working hard, but our test scores are stuck at the bottom of the barrel. The quick fixes we've tried haven't worked and are creating an atmosphere of frustration and defensiveness.

Organize Opportunities to Harness the Collective Wisdom of the Faculty

Shawn: We had an amazing experience at our school last year. Our principal read a book called *Taking Charge: Leading With Passion and Purpose in the Principalship.*[4] It's worth buying and reading. He had us all read Chapter 3 "Using Classroom Evidence for Learning, Capacity-Building, and Accountability." Then he went through the same process the author Paul Shaw describes in the chapter called "Initiating Collective Professional Learning and Development."

Shamele: What process?

Shawn: Clarence, the principal, committed one afternoon a week to personally teaching the school's most difficult class. He posted a large sheet of paper on the faculty room wall and divided it into two columns ... on the top of one he wrote, "What I did." and on the other "What the students did." At a staff meeting he described the lesson he taught and filled in the two columns. Clarence had attempted to use one of the cooperative learning strategies the staff had been studying: "Think-Pair-Share." His chart looked like this.

What I did:

I asked students to brainstorm what they knew about the Canadian Shield, the topic of the geography lesson.

What students did:

They all talked at once, interrupted and corrected one another.

What I did:

I asked them to pair up and discuss what they wanted to learn.

What students did:

They argued because they didn't want to work with a particular person.

What I did:

I asked them to get in groups of three or four to discuss what they'd learned.

What students did:

They seemed confused.

Shawn: The lesson was a disaster, but his staff was impressed that Clarence was willing to take a risk. Many teachers had suggestions that might have improved the lesson. So Clarence added another column "What I Learned."

Shamele: Then what?

Shawn: Clarence reviewed a few more of his own lessons incorporating what he learned from the teachers' suggestions. Then he asked for volunteers to do the same. At first only a few brave souls volunteered, but after they reported having learned so much and actually enjoying the process, more teachers presented lessons.

Shamele: That would take a lot of guts. But I can see it would be powerful. We'd have to build a lot of trust for folks to expose their goof-ups. But we're always talking to kids about learning from their mistakes and learning from each other. It might be useful to go through the process ourselves.

Shawn: There's no better learning experience. It lifts everyone's boat, both the presenters and those making suggestions. Our principal did the same thing at our school with the same results. The teachers at Clarence's school kept adding new columns. So did we ... with headings like:

- What I intended
- What happened
- How engaged were students
- Who wasn't engaged
- What was the kind and quality of student interactions
- What did students learn and how do you know
- Questions I have
- What I'm still curious about

Shamele: We've had all sorts of consultants working to fix us. Many of their ideas sound good on paper but never quite work the way they're intended. I wonder if it's because we didn't ask these simple questions first.

Shawn*:* I think asking simple questions often creates deeper and more practical learning than quick fixes supplied by outside consultants. It's the process of making our practice public and working together that's important. We often act like private contractors, working alone, covering up or not even recognizing our mistakes. So, we're unable to learn from them. It's curious. We're teachers. We know a lot about the theory of learning, but we rarely apply it to ourselves. We're better and more effective when we work together to help one another grow. We needed a way to tap into the collective wisdom that already existed in our faculty. The example from Paul Shaw's book got us started.

Shamele: I want to help our faculty move from private contractors to a cohesive learning organization. You've given me some ideas to get started.

Shawn: There's no quick fix. It takes courage and persistence. But it's the only growth I've experienced that's empowering and sustainable.

Getting started is hard. Our principal helped by complimenting teachers' willingness to present a lesson to the group. He did this orally at staff meetings, in private, and in writing on teacher evaluations. He was telling us our willingness to learn and help our colleagues learn was more important to him than a perfect lesson. *Mistakes that were exposed and used as a springboard to learning were more valuable than a perfect lesson* (which doesn't exist anyway). The old "dog and pony shows" we used to put on when the principal came to observe disappeared. In their place were real learning opportunities.

These learning sessions we now have monthly at our regularly scheduled staff meeting have transformed our school. Although we haven't concentrated specifically on test scores, as teaching improves and learning increases, our test score have gradually risen.

Six months later

Shawn: We haven't talked for a while. What's up?

Shamele: All kinds of things. I've been itching to talk to you.

Shawn: Shoot.

Shamele: I taught a lesson myself and analyzed it at a staff meeting using the columns "What I did" and "What the students did." Just as in Paul Shaw's book teachers gave me suggestions about how to improve my lesson and I added a third column "What I Learned." Everyone was engaged and seemed to really enjoy the exercise, but when I asked for volunteers, no one came forward. So I did it again, and still no one came forward.

Shawn: What did you do?

Shamele: I privately asked a couple of veteran teachers if they would be willing to present lessons. They said okay. It was easier to be picked than to volunteer. I also told the non-tenured teachers I'm evaluating this year, if they would present a lesson to the staff I would consider it one of the three observations I was mandated to do for their evaluation. I said I would look favorably on any non-tenured teacher who was willing to present a lesson. I thought if one or two people got the ball rolling, the rest would follow.

Shawn: Did it work?

Shamele: It did. After veteran teachers, a few brave non-tenured teachers stepped forward. They got a lot of praise from me and said they actually enjoyed the process and learned a lot. I kept the sessions short. I allotted about 15 minutes for each one on the regular staff meeting agenda. I think this made them more palatable and to the point. We didn't have time to get off on tangents and the presenting teacher walked away with a few interesting suggestions instead of a long list of changes she needed to make. It's only been a few months but the process is beginning to pick up momentum.

Shawn: Did you make any ground rules? Like the audience had to say what they liked about the lesson before they made suggestions for change.

Shamele: I thought about it. I wondered if I should rule out any negative statements like "You shouldn't have ..." But in the end I decided to let things flow naturally and see what happens. I trusted the staff to behave appropriately and productively.

Shawn: Did they?

Shamele: Yes. Instead of making rules I decided to model the behavior I thought would be most productive. So I frequently said, things like "I noticed every student in the class was engaged in the discussion" or "Why did you decide to check for understanding so frequently?"

After a while, I started to hear my words spoken as we reviewed more lessons. I think it was better than establishing rules.

Shawn: So do I. Good call. Where are you now?

Shamele: We're on our way. I hope more and more folks will see the benefit of sharing lessons as we learn to trust the process and one another. As we mine the tremendous amount of experience and professional know-how that exists in our faculty, we'll build our collective capacity to meet our students' learning needs. I also hope this learning will be reflected in the higher test scores the state department of education is looking for.

Shawn: You've taken this idea and run with it. I think you're on your way to building a strong staff with sophisticated teaching skills ... the kind that really make a difference in student learning. You're developing a strong learning culture for teachers, students, and yourself.

Test Scores

Shamele: Do you have time to discuss test scores? I love the stuff we've been talking about and I think it will be powerful in the long run, but I'm worried about test scores this year.

Shawn: Here's what we did about test scores. First we looked over the data we had on our test scores and noticed that many of our students gave up when they ran into two or three questions they couldn't answer. So we:

- talked about probability, explaining that they'd get zero answers right if they didn't try and would probably get a few right if they gave them their best guess;
- taught them to mark the questions they couldn't answer, complete the rest, then go back to the marked questions;
- talked about persistence, sticking with a task until it's complete even if you run into obstacles;
- put one quick problem or question in the test format on the board every morning in every classroom for several months so students got used to the test format.

None of this interfered with our everyday instruction that was focused on deeper understanding. It was not a substitute for the more substantive changes in teaching and learning we'd been talking about, but it did give us a real boost in our test scores and taught students about probability and persistence, important life lessons.

Shamele: That sounds pretty easy.

Shawn: Not as easy as it sounds. There were teachers who were opposed to what they called "teaching to the test." Others felt we weren't teaching to the test at all. Just teaching test-taking skills that allowed students to show what they really knew. The principal weighed in with a political argument. He said the central office, the state department, etc. were less likely to try to fix us while we were working to build our capacity, if our test scores were decent. Everyone agreed with that.

Shamele: I love the idea of building capacity rather than looking for quick fixes. I think it's a foundation on which we can build a great school. I also think our students need help with test-taking skills. You've given me ideas about how to get started with both.

Conclusion

Attempting to fix people involves doing something *to* them. Building capacity involves doing something *with* them. The first creates pushback and results in superficial and temporary improvement. The second takes longer but creates a positive momentum that feeds on itself and results in substantial, long-lasting, and continual growth both for individuals and the school as a whole.

Strategies for Becoming a Reflective Leader

Reading

Read the first three chapters of *Mindset* with your staff.

Journaling/Collective Wisdom

Write about the teaching and learning mindsets:

- you grew up with;
- you currently hold;
- any inconsistencies between your current mindsets and practice at your school;
- mindsets and practices that need strengthening;
- mindsets and practice that need changing.

Organize a staff meeting agenda around the same questions you asked yourself.
Ask teachers to journal and discuss:

- three ways our current practice encourages continual improvement;
- how their beliefs about teaching and learning are connected to their current pedagogical practices.

Practice new behaviors

Hold one-on-one or small group conferences with teachers. Ask them to bring an artifact that illustrates something they're proud of, struggling with, or puzzled by. Use these as springboards for conversations about teaching and learning.

Observing Classroom Practice

Observe classroom practice and discuss observations with teachers. Have teachers observe other teachers. Instead of focusing these observation conversations on what teachers are doing right or wrong, ask questions that help teachers think more deeply about their practice. Include questions about why they made particular decisions, what the outcome of those decisions was, and how a different decision might have produced a different outcome.

Citations

1. Carol Dweck, *Mindset: The New Psychology of Success* (New York, NY: Ballantine Books, 2006).

2. Peter Senge et al., *Presence: Human Purpose and the Field of the Future* (Cambridge, MA: Society for Organizational Learning, 2004).
3. Lee Jenkins, *From Systems Thinking to Systemic Action* (Lanham, MD: Rowman & Littlefield Education, 2008).
4. Paul Shaw, *Taking Charge: Leading With Passion and Purpose in the Principalship* (New York, NY: Teachers College Press, 2012).

Additional Reading

Donald Schoen, *Educating the Reflective Practitioner* (New York, NY: Jossey-Bass Inc., 1983).

4 Building a Competent, Cohesive Faculty

The Whole Is Bigger Than the Sum of Its Parts

In one school, teachers resist change and blame students, parents, or administrators for failure. In another, they take responsibility for every student's learning, and expect to continually improve their practice. In the first school, each teacher is an independent contractor who develops her expertise separate from her colleagues. In the second, teachers work and learn together to challenge the status quo and nurture one another's growth. As a result, a synergy develops and the whole becomes larger than the sum of the parts.

There are good teachers in both schools, but students in the second get a consistently, better education. The difference is culture. In this chapter, principals and their mentors discuss ways to create a culture that fuels great teaching and produces outstanding schools.

Building such a culture requires principals who are lead learners in a community of learners. Energy and efficacy permeate these schools. Their principals are clearly focused on student learning, inspire others to do their best work, and are always learning themselves. They accept responsibility for creating a learning space where continual growth takes place. This means:

- setting boundaries by moving teachers on who are unwilling or unable to meet their standards of excellence;
- working with teachers to create a demanding and clear process for interviewing, hiring, developing, and evaluating teachers;
- inspiring teachers to set and reach high standards of excellence;
- establishing an ethos of continual improvement;

- creating a learning environment that balances safety and challenge;
- helping teachers learn together and support one another's growth;
- involving teachers in decisions that affect their practice and the learning culture of the school.

Creating a Clear Process for Interviewing, Hiring, Developing, and Evaluating Teachers

Principal: Kyle is the new principal at Oakville Middle School
Mentor: Catherine is a retired principal assigned to Kyle as a mentor

Catherine: Let's talk about interviewing, hiring, developing, and evaluating teachers. We should also discuss the hardest of all … letting teachers go.

Hiring Teachers

Catherine: Start with a faculty conversation about the characteristics you want in every faculty member. Answering this question will help teachers examine their own development and take responsibility for shaping the whole faculty. Then talk about more specific characteristics you want in a particular position with a smaller team that will be working closely with that teacher.

Kyle: How would you organize that conversation?

Catherine: Review the standards your district has set for teachers. Then I'd have a brainstorming session at a regular staff meeting and use dot voting to set priorities for the most important characteristics.

Kyle: What characteristics did you look for?

Catherine: The rock bottom characteristics I looked for in every teacher are: 1) She is able to see the world through someone else's eyes, and 2) She has an insatiable desire to learn and improve. Teachers who are unable to see the world from others' viewpoints tend to focus on what they're teaching rather that what students are learning. And teachers who don't have a strong desire to learn and improve stagnate and become resistant to change.

When we had a vacancy, I formed an interview team consisting of teachers at the grade level or in the department where the new teacher will work. I included a specialist or someone from a different area for another perspective. We met for one half hour before the interview and looked at the list of characteristics the staff developed adding any additional characteristics for this particular position.

I worked with a principal who skipped the prioritizing step. Her primary goal was to hire more qualified African-American teachers so the faculty would mirror the student body. Because she failed to have teachers set priorities before the interview, the group voted for an equally qualified white candidate. The principal over-ruled their decision and hired the African-American candidate. The principal eroded the interviewing teachers' trust and put the new teacher in a difficult position. This could have been avoided by setting a priority of racially balancing the faculty before interviewing candidates.

After you develop a list of characteristics and prioritize them, craft questions that allow you to ascertain if the candidate possesses those qualities. Two of my favorites are:

Desired Characteristics: candidate takes responsibility for the learning of all students and is continually learning himself.

Question: What do you feel proudest of in your career so far?

Listen for: A story of single student or group of students who struggled with a lesson and what the teacher did to reach those students.

Follow-up Questions: What did you learn from those students? What did they learn from you? In the same situation again, what would you do differently?

Red Flags: The candidate focuses on his own accomplishments rather than those of students. "I finished my master's degree." or "I was selected as teacher of the year."

Candidate blames others for his lack of success and fails to keep searching for ways to reach all his students.

Desired Characteristics: candidate takes responsibility for solving problems, builds a repertoire of problem-solving strategies, and is able to view situations from another's viewpoint.

Question: What is the most difficult situation you've encountered, what did you do to solve the problem, and what did you learn from this situation?

Listen for: Candidate describes the situation without blaming others or complaining about circumstances. She understands others viewpoint even if she disagrees with them. She learns from this situation and talks about applying what she learns to other situations. She maintains focus on individual student learning.

Red Flags: Candidate blames others for the situation and loses focus on individual student's learning

Ask questions that get the candidate talking about his/her practice. If you listen carefully without interjecting your own ideas, candidates will tell you exactly who they are. Ask short questions and let the interviewee do most of the talking.

Developing Teachers

Catherine: In some schools, there are teachers who make the grade and are left alone to do their own thing. Professional development is seen as remediation for everyone else. It takes place only on staff development days separate from the rest of teachers' practice.

In other schools, there is the expectation of teacher learning and professional development is focused on continual improvement, not remediation. Teachers in these schools are expected to meet minimum standards but those standards are only a beginning. Evaluation is based on developing an ever more sophisticated practice. All conversations a teacher has with colleagues, the principal, students, and parents become professional development opportunities. Teachers are expected to reflect on and learn from these interactions. Mistakes are exposed and seen as opportunities to learn.

Kyle: Where do those standards come from? How can I measure continual learning?

Catherine: Good questions. They come from national, state, and school districts standards. The trick is to help faculties build on these broad standards to develop their own specific standards. If the faculty is growing together, their standards will become increasingly more sophisticated and nuanced.

How principals talk to teachers has a powerful effect on their development. If you talk about what they're learning and how their learning affects their practice, teachers will become reflective. If you pose provocative questions like, "I notice several students seemed confused. What are your plans for them?" "Is there something else you need to learn to reach them?" you'll create the expectation of learning and continual improvement. This creates a different culture and different expectations than simply listing a teacher's strengths and weaknesses at the end of the year. It's also a powerful incentive to mention a teacher's learning and it's connection to his practice in your written evaluation.

Measuring continual growth requires asking good questions, making careful observations, and reviewing data. It's important to measure output (what students are learning) rather than input (teacher presented learning activities). I've worked in districts where teachers list all the workshops they've attended without regard to how their learning affected their practice. I'd rather have a teacher read one book or attend one workshop that really improves her practice, than read many books or attend a lot of workshops that have little or no effect on their practice.

Kyle: Sounds great—and difficult. I'll need to be learning with the teachers. I'm hoping you'll be around for guidance.

Catherine: Of course. Begin by paying attention to the way you talk to teachers. Every conversation is an opportunity to shape a culture. Begin by journaling about conversations you have with teachers and noting how your responses furthered (or failed to further) a culture of continual learning.

Moving Teachers On

Kyle: We have a conscientious group of teachers who are eager to improve their practice and work well with one another. However, there are two I'm concerned about. One who's been here a long time and has a following of favorite students and parents with whom he curries favor. From what I can tell, other students are left to flounder. His focus is on what he is teaching, not what the students are learning. He hasn't improved his pedagogical skills for a long time. Nor does he seem interested in doing so. When I observe, there is very little of substance to record. When I talk to him about his lessons, I get pat answers that reveal little understanding of or interest in his students or their learning.

The other person is a third year teacher who continues to struggle with classroom management and doesn't have a solid grasp of the curriculum. I'm not sure she has the ability or interest to keep up with the work we're doing at Oakville Middle School.

When I think about how much time and effort it would take to bring them up to speed, the number of students who are getting a mediocre education in their classrooms, and the opportunity costs when there are so many excellent teachers looking for jobs, I'd really like to counsel them out. I might be able to do that with the non-tenured teacher but with the tenured teacher, I'm not so sure.

Catherine: This is the hardest and most important responsibility a principal has. By setting limits on what is acceptable professional behavior you create a defined learning space in which institutional growth thrives. Without these limits, when everything and anything is acceptable, the space becomes too diffuse for meaningful group learning to take place.

Kyle: That sounds serious.

Catherine: It is. It's the reason many schools wallow in mediocrity despite the best efforts of many teachers.

Kyle: What should I do?

Catherine: Begin by being clear about your expectations. Tell these teachers that their teaching needs to change in some profound ways. Clearly outline these changes and your expectations, being as specific as possible about the time and energy this will require. Ask them to think about whether they're interested in undertaking the work these changes will require.

Give them a week to think about their personal goals and how they fit with the changes you expect. Tell them if they decide they don't want to change, you'll help them move on. If they decide to change you'll work with them to reach the new standards. Reiterate the learning, time, and energy these changes will require. You'll have to convince them you're serious and you'll be around to implement the changes. Many teachers have seen principals come and go and simply wait them out. This attitude breeds cynicism that is toxic to growth.

If this choice is presented in a serious way without sugar coating the difficulties that lie ahead, many teachers will decide to leave of their own accord. If not, you've created a framework for future work with them. They know this won't be business as usual. If they decide to stay, work with them to bring them up to the new standards. If that doesn't work, begin your school's process for terminating teachers. This is a tough, but essential process to initiate. Two things have helped me ramp up my courage.

First, I used the "Who pays?" test. When I reminded myself of the number of students who were paying and would pay in the future for subpar instruction, when I remembered that I was the only one who could address this issue, and when I realized the drag on the rest of the staff poor instruction caused, I developed the courage to have these difficult conversations. Second, I called a friend or mentor and told them when I planned the conversation and told them I'd call when it was over. This kept me from backing down or being less firm than I intended.

You'll be surprised what a strong and positive effect it has on the entire staff when you set clear boundaries about the standards of teaching in your school and back them up with action.

Inspiring Teachers

Catherine: Change is difficult. It requires an expansion of spirit, possibilities, and capabilities. *Inspirational leadership is the energy that fuels this expansion.* John Stanford was a major general in the army. When he retired, he became the superintendent of the Seattle Public Schools… an unusual choice for military retirement. But he was a guy on a mission. He felt that many of the leadership skills he had learned in the armed forces could apply to education. He wrote a book entitled *Victory in Our Schools* in which he said soldiers were folks who signed up to give their lives for their country.[1] They weren't there for the money. They were motivated by a sense of honor and purpose. Stanford thought this described teachers as well. Most teachers enter the profession with a strong sense of mission. Inspirational leaders that tap into that mission give teachers the energy and optimism they need to continually reach for higher levels of excellence. Leadership that only focuses only on rules and skills limits the striving for excellence that characterizes great schools.

Kyle: So how does a person become an inspirational leader? I've always thought of myself as a pretty competent guy, but I'm kind of low key. I don't see myself as charismatic.

Catherine: You don't have to be flamboyant, or an extrovert to be an inspirational leader. Folks draw more inspiration from sincerity and example than from self-promotion.

Kyle: What does that mean?

Catherine: It means having high aspirations for yourself and the courage to be transparent about your learning, doubts, and decisions. It means learning along with your teachers and sharing your struggles as you embark on a learning journey together.

Development is not something you do *to* teachers, it's something you do *with* them. Just as you expect them to continually grow more competent and sophisticated as they move through their careers, you expect the same of yourself. Your growth facilitates theirs and vice versa. Instead of you fixing them, you all grow together. This creates the optimism, energy, and motivation behind great schools. All interactions you have with teachers and they have with one another are opportunities for inspiration. Optimism and inspiration is communicable diseases.

Kyle: Can you give me some examples?

What You Notice

Catherine: Most important is *to notice what you notice*. What you notice and comment on will be the things teachers repeat. When you see a teacher going out of her way to help a struggling student, do you comment? Do you notice a veteran teacher helping a new teacher and do you comment?

When a teacher makes a particularly useful remark in a staff meeting, do you notice and comment on that? The first step is to notice what you notice. The second is to think about those things you're not noticing. Your noticing and comments are powerful tools for building the kind of learning culture you're working towards. Noticing can take the form of appreciation, questioning, or empathy. If done honestly, frequently and with the goal of promoting growth it has a powerful effect on your school culture. You'll know the culture is growing when you hear teachers noticing and talking to one another, the way you're noticing and talking to them.

An outstanding principal I had the privilege of mentoring carries noticing a step farther. He calls it "Recognizing Our Own." Teachers are asked at the beginning of every staff meeting to report on a teaching strategy they've observed a colleague using. This simple exercise has reinforced a culture of continual learning and made the collective wisdom of the faculty available to everyone.

Kyle: I think I'll journal about what I'm noticing and commenting on.

Catherine: Great idea. You might also want to think about what you're not noticing. That's more difficult, but asking another teacher to partner with you for an observation, or asking the teacher you're observing what you missed can help.

Developing an Ethos of Continual Improvement

Catherine: Continual improvement begins with a balance of safety and challenge. Teachers need to feel safe enough to take the risks new enterprises and new learning require and, at the same time, be continually challenged to upgrade their practice. This is a delicate balance that is more like riding a bicycle than balancing on a scale ... a dynamic process always in need of adjustment. Leaning too far in either direction will cause a problem. Too much risk, teachers will shut down and resist change. Too much safety, growth will stagnate. Continual improvement requires a constant rebalancing of safety and challenge.

Kyle: Continual improvement makes sense, but sounds exhausting ... like a race without a finish line. I wonder if it would be helpful to celebrate the journey itself and some markers along the way.

Catherine: Great idea! Your job is to make sure teachers have the energy and optimism to continue the journey.

In an enterprise as complex as school improvement, there are bound to be mistakes. In fact, no mistakes may mean too little risk. If mistakes are viewed as failures and are hidden little learning takes place. If they are viewed as learning opportunities, they become the fuel for continual improvement. The military does a particularly good job of learning from mistakes. After any significant enterprise, they hold an "after action review." A group of people involved in the enterprise meet and review what went well, what didn't, and what could be done differently next time. When after action reviews are woven into the fabric of every endeavor you and your faculty undertake, they create a culture of continual improvement.

Kyle: We just had our fall curriculum night for parents. I think I'll put an after action review on the agenda for our next staff meeting.

Catherine: Another important tool for building a culture of continual improvement is what you expect of yourself. Your own example provides a template and challenge for everyone else. This means making self-examination and admitting and learning from mistakes a regular part of your practice. It means learning from teachers as well as them learning from you.

Kyle: I'm afraid teachers might lose respect for me. After all, I'm supposed to be the expert.

Catherine: I worried about that too. But the opposite happened. When I moved from an expert to a lead learner, I got more respect. The teachers and I became colleagues in a mutual endeavor for which we were all responsible. When responsibility and transparency were spread widely throughout the staff, we all became more powerful. That included me.

Learning and Growing Together

Catherine: In the great schools I worked in, teachers worked together to inspire one another to continually improve their practice. They took responsibility for the education all their students received throughout their tenure at their school. This meant the second grade teacher was interested in what happens to students in the fifth grade and the English teacher wants his students to become proficient in math. Successful principals create this expectation.

Kyle: How do you do that?

Catherine: I've noticed in schools where everyone is learning and growing together, principal and teachers use the term "we" when referring to the faculty. They rarely use the first or third person avoiding an "us and them" mentality. Notice when you include yourself by using "we."

The second is how principals structure meetings and make decisions. In growth oriented schools meetings are used for mutual learning and decision-making. In my school, we agreed to use e-mail, the weekly staff memo, and other venues for announcements and feedback. We learned protocols that enabled us to maximize the time we had together without prolonging our meetings.

A tool we used frequently was round robin sharing. For example, before a curriculum night with parents, we went around the circle (we always sat in a circle) and asked everyone for a two-minute idea of something they'd planned for the evening. The idea was to share and learn together rather than hoarding good ideas to make yourself a star. We talked about ourselves as a repertory theater group rather than a few stars and the rest bit players. We wanted to create a rising tide that floated everyone's boat.

Kyle: I can't imagine my star teachers will want to give up their star status.

Catherine: It depends on what you expect, notice, and reward. Most star teachers find it more interesting and rewarding to work with a faculty that's learning together and most teachers want what's best for their students. It may take a while and you will have to be persistent but when they see the benefit to students of a faculty that's learning and growing together, they'll be sold.

The way you and your faculty make decisions provides the underpinning for a competent and cohesive faculty, especially in areas that directly affect their work with students. I think we should devote a couple of conversations to meetings and making decisions. There are a few questions you may want to ask yourself until then.

- Who makes which decisions?
- Is the process for making decisions clear and transparent to everyone?
- Are teachers aware of the reasons for making particular decisions?
- Do teachers feel a collective sense of openness, honesty, and accomplishment?

Conclusion

Culture is like the air we breathe. It's not always visible, but it's all around us and influences everything we do. Great principals consciously work to build a culture that encourages collaboration, continual growth, and group responsibility. They do this by involving teachers in setting boundaries for acceptable practice, and interviewing and developing their colleagues. They inspire teachers to reach high standards of excellence, establish an ethos of continual improvement, and create a learning environment that balances safety and challenge. They help teachers learn together, support one another's growth, and make group decisions that affect their practice and the learning culture of the school.

Strategies for Becoming a Reflective Leader

Collective Wisdom

Work with teachers to develop standards of practice. Give them material your district publishes on desirable teacher traits and background. Ask them to read articles such as *Teachers Hiring Teachers* by Mary Clement.[2] Then use brainstorming and dot voting to establish a list of standards for your school.

Include teachers on interview teams. Spend time before each interview establishing the traits and experience you're looking for in a candidate, establishing priorities, and thinking about questions that reveal this information. Be clear upfront about the role teachers will play in the interview process. Either, you will make the final decision and their input will advise your decision; or they will make the final decision either with a majority vote or a consensus.

Involve teachers in their own and their colleagues' professional growth by having them observe one another, participate in small group conversations about student work and large group conversations about pedagogy and the day-to-day operations of the school.

Initiate the practice of "Recognizing Our Own" at the beginning of staff meetings.

Journaling/Talking with Mentor/Practicing New Behaviors

Use the standards of practice you developed with your staff and those set by your school district to evaluate teachers. When a teacher fails to meet these standards, outline the changes you expect. Be clear about your intentions. Give them two choices: leave of their own volition or stay and work with you to meet these standards. If they choose the second option, work with them to meet the standards. Begin termination proceedings if the standards aren't met in a timely fashion.

It helps to use your journal and your mentor to get clear about your intentions, expectations, and process. Before and after a conversation with this teacher divide your journal in three columns 1) What you said or intended to say 2) What the teacher might say or said, and 3) Your feelings, thinking, and responses. Discuss these with your mentor before and after you meet with the teacher. Because these are difficult conversations, it helps to arrange to call your mentor when the conversation is over. Deciding "Who Pays?" and understanding that any enterprise is defined by its boundaries should bolster your courage.

Record three ways in which you have:

- involved teachers in making decisions that affect their practice and the learning culture of the school;
- furthered the idea of continual improvement;
- created an environment for learning that balanced safety and challenge.

Citations

1. John Stanford, *Victory in Our Schools* (New York, NY: Bantam Books, 1999).
2. Mary C. Clement, "Teachers Hiring Teachers," *Educational Leadership* 7:2 (2013).

Additional Reading

Linda Lambert, *Leadership Capacity for Lasting School Improvement* (Alexandria, VA: Association for Supervision and Curriculum Development, 2003).

Paul Shaw, *Taking Charge: Leading With Passion and Purpose in the Principalship* (New York, NY: Teachers College Press, 2012).

5 Building a Collegial Culture

No More Insiders and Outsiders

In many schools, teachers work as independent contractors. Each teacher closes his classroom door and teaches as he sees best. There is a strong emphasis on teacher autonomy and little sense of a common purpose. When teachers work independently and have few opportunities to learn from or plan with one another, learning and growth are stifled, and energy and optimism are in short supply. Schools like this may have great teachers but they never become great schools.

Lacking a sense of belonging to a larger purpose, teachers form cliques. A balkanized culture develops and people begin to protect their own turf. One clique is the in-group. They have the principal's ear and are perceived to have more power than others. Another clique clings to the status quo and subtly sabotages reform efforts. Yet another sees themselves as the only ones who really care about all the students. Because teachers only talk to other people in their clique, these attitudes are frequently reinforced and rarely challenged.

When principals provide no other means of communication, teachers rely on gossip to find out what's happening. This breeds a culture of mistrust that's toxic to growth and development. A principal's behavior and policies (or lack of policies) can unintentionally reinforce such a culture.

In this chapter, principals and their mentors explore ways to develop a positive collegial culture by providing many ways for teachers to learn and work together to improve teaching throughout the school. This includes how:

- information is disseminated;
- resources are allocated;
- problems are solved.

Building a School-Wide Learning Culture

Principal: Kyle is the new principal of Oakville Middle School
Mentor: Catherine is a retired principal assigned to Kyle as a mentor

Kyle: I have a notebook full of stories and questions I'm eager to discuss with you. The first time we met we talked about building trust. I thought I was a pretty trustworthy guy and couldn't understand why it wasn't apparent to everyone. You taught me that being trustworthy was the foundation of building trust but it wasn't enough. You said I needed to project my trustworthiness by thinking out loud. That simple practice has made a significant difference in my ability to get things done at school and at home as well. I thank you for that.

Now I have a different trust problem. It's about teachers trusting one another. Teachers' schedules are tight. They have few opportunities to interact with more than a small circle of colleagues who share a similar location in the building or a similar teaching assignment. Often they share similar opinions and even when they don't, they hesitate to contradict one another. This inhibits the free exchange of ideas and breeds mistrust, making it difficult to create a dynamic learning culture.

Catherine: Often the systems and procedures that divide people are the very ones that can be used to unite them. We should talk about:

- how people know what's going on around here;
- how they get the things they need;
- how and with whom they solve problems;
- what opportunities they have to learn from one another.

How Information Is Disseminated

Catherine: Let's start with how folks know what's going on around here. In most schools there are formal and informal channels of communication. Formal communication includes memos, newsletters, staff agendas, etc. usually shared with the whole staff or a large group. Informal communication is what folks talk about over lunch, in the parking lot, and over drinks on Friday afternoon. It's usually shared one-on-one or with a small group of like-minded friends. This information may or may not be accurate, but it has a powerful impact on the learning culture of a school. The trick is to move as much information as possible out of the informal column to the formal side so everyone knows what's going on all the time. Information is power. Everyone knowing the same information at the same time discourages in-groups and out-groups and separates fact from fiction, two conditions necessary to build a productive collegial culture.

Kyle: How do I begin?

Catherine: You begin with clear, well-written, widely circulated, and regularly disseminated communication venues such as a weekly staff memo.

Kyle: We already do that.

Catherine: Good. Let's take a look and see if your weekly memo meets my criteria.

- **Is it clear and well written?** Weekly memos from the principal are often thought of as an irritating detail to be dashed off at the last minute. I don't think they have to be the great American novel, but they need to be user friendly so everyone actually reads them. Weekly memos should be short and to the point. Information most important to teachers should come first.
- I used to begin my weekly memos with an **all-school calendar for the week**. At a glance teachers were able to get a picture of all the school's activities for the week. That way they knew how their activities fit into the whole.
- Next came **important announcements**.
- Sometimes I included **my thinking on a topic or recognition for someone,** but I always tried to keep it to one or two paragraphs. This section became a kind of thinking out loud in writing.
- I included the **agenda for the next staff meeting** so people could be thinking about or gathering materials for the topics we would be discussing. This made for more thoughtful discussions and enabled teachers to make additions or suggestions to enhance the agenda.

The hardest part was being an editor ... for myself and other people. I cut out unnecessary prepositional phrases, adverbs, long run-on sentences, and interesting but non-essential information. When folks gave me pieces to include in the weekly newsletter, I would edit them not to change content but to keep them short and to the point. If they couldn't be shortened, I'd ask the author to use another venue to disseminate the information. My goal was to keep the memo easily accessible so that teachers actually read it. I wanted everyone to start each week with all the information they needed to be productive members of our school community. They needed to know what was going on throughout the school without being burdened with extraneous information.

Kyle: I'm afraid I've been guilty of just dashing off these memos without much thought or asking my secretary to type all the announcements everyone gives her. Frankly, I'm not sure I have time for much more.

Catherine: I understand. Remember the story about Mark Twain who apologized for sending a long letter to a friend. He said he didn't have time to write a short one. I wonder if you might develop a format, perhaps consulting with a group of teachers or asking for ideas and feedback from everyone. For example, calendar first, short announcements next, then staff agenda or something like that. Once the format is established, you could turn the job of assembling the memo over to your secretary with instructions to keep it short and to the point. You should do a final editing yourself.

The goal is to keep the weekly memo user friendly and everyone in the loop about what's happening throughout the school. You want to avoid a situation where an absence of information creates a vacuum that gets filled with gossip and inaccurate information.

Kyle: I wonder if it I should put a limit on the number of pages. Our last memo was more than five pages long. I doubt anyone read the whole thing. Maybe no more than two pages. Putting a limit on the number of pages would force us to set priorities.

Catherine: Good idea. The friendly advice from the nurse or counselor might have to be shortened or find another venue.

Kyle: It might cause some ruffled feathers at first, but I think a shorter, more concise memo would be more effective.

Catherine: My other two criteria were to publish the memo regularly so folks could count on it and to distribute it widely so all staff members have the same information at the same time.

Kyle: I think we publish our memo fairly regularly and distribute it to everyone although I'm not positive about either of these. I'll check. Until we talked, I didn't think it was that important.

Catherine: The other thing that helped us get rid of in-groups and out-groups was how I handled folks who came to my office to talk about an issue. Unless the issue was private and pertained only to them, I would suggest they put it on the staff meeting agenda or include it in the weekly memo. After a while, folks stopped asking for individual sessions with me. If they thought the issue was important and pertained to the whole school, they put it directly on the agenda or in the newsletter. If it pertained to only one other person, I suggested they handle the issue directly with that person. This eliminated a lot of gossip, built trust, discouraged one person from speaking for others, and dispelled the myth of principal's favorites.

Kyle: There are a few staff members who want to tell me about situations with other teachers that they think need my attention. They mean well, but they put me in an uncomfortable position. I haven't known how to handle them. What you're suggesting sounds so simple. Just say no.

Catherine: Yes, but also direct them to take responsibility for solving the problem themselves or include the whole staff in the solution. Principals need to be gathering information about what's happening at their school. They face complex problems they need to sort through by talking to someone who's a good listener and understands the situation. It's tempting to make a teacher who comes to your office with information and understanding a confidant. But it's always a mistake ... much better to use the staff as a whole or an outside mentor for this information and understanding. I can't tell you how many stories I've heard about a confidant who becomes an in-group of one and erodes the trust and collegiality throughout the school.

Kyle: That was the case in the last school I worked. The principal meant well, but there was always a perception of favoritism and an undercurrent of mistrust.

How Resources Are Allocated

Catherine: Let's talk about how resources are allocated. It's difficult to develop a supportive collegial culture if the allocation of resources is perceived as unfair. The reality or even the perception that some teachers are getting more favorable treatment than others works against a collegial culture. A plan that is transparent and inclusive brings the wisdom of the whole staff to bear on these decisions and promotes a spirit of collegiality.

In my school, we were asking a good deal more from teachers than we had in the past. Even though most of them liked the changes we were making, many felt uncertain and overburdened. We were giving students greater control over their learning—perhaps teachers needed greater control of their work. At the time I was reading *Leadership and The New Science* by Margaret Wheatley.[1] She said patterns of behavior organize cultures, just as patterns organize nature. I hoped that one of our patterns would be more control and more responsibility at every level.

I think the way we allocated resources was the single most important thing we did to move our culture from dependence to collaboration and our staff from balkanized to a collegial culture.

Kyle: You've given me a lot to think about and some things I'd like to put in place fairly soon. Could we meet next month and talk about how we disseminate information at Oakville Middle School and how we might allocate resources for next year?

Catherine: Sounds good. I'd also like to talk about ways to solve problems that help build a supportive collegial culture. Do some journaling about the problems you encounter between now and our next meeting.

Kyle: We have a little more time today. Can you tell me what you mean by how problems are solved?

How Problems Are Solved

Catherine: Sure. I think the most important problem-solving criteria for building a collegial culture is who to include in the solving process.

My goal is to be as inclusive as possible. I think it's particularly important to include as many of the people who will be affected by the solution as possible. A teacher I worked with some years ago recalled this story. It illustrates the power of including folks in the problem-solving process.

We arrived at school on a cloudy day in May with a forecast for afternoon showers. We needed to decide whether to go ahead with our plans for an all-school field day at the high school football field, curtail the activities and move them to our school playground, or cancel field day all together. I called a quick stand-up meeting of the staff. We had a short discussion, took a vote, and decided to go ahead with our field day plans with some adjustments to the timing and an altered bus schedule. The altered plan worked well, the rain held off until later in the day, and everyone had a good time.

The teacher said the exact same situation arose with another principal. He handled the situation differently. He made the same decision we did, to hold the track meet at the high school field as planned with an altered bus schedule. His solution was the same, but his problem-solving process was different. He didn't want to bother teachers with a trivial decision so he decided himself. She said, "It was a mess. Nothing went right." The difference, according to her, was that I involved the entire staff in the decision. And although the solution was the same, the execution was different. Because it was their decision, teachers felt responsible for making it work. They made many small adjustments throughout the day that made it a success. Adjustments teachers failed to make when the decision wasn't theirs.

Kyle: A cautionary tale. But you can't involve everyone in every decision; how do you know which ones to make yourself and in which one's to include others?

Catherine: That's the art of leadership. First I decide who will be directly impacted by the solution to a problem. Then I try to figure out a way to include as many of these people as possible in finding a solution to the problem. If possible, it's best to get all these folks in the same room at the same time like I did with the quick stand-up meeting before field day. If that's not feasible, I try to find another way for them to provide input. This broadens the number of people who are in the loop of what's happening and greatly enriches the problem-solving process by helping us view a problem from various perspectives, offer a wider array of possible solutions, and spread ownership and responsibly over a larger group.

Kyle: Can you give me some examples?

Catherine: Sure. Once we began asking ourselves, "Who's missing?" we regularly included:

- parents in our student study team meetings;
- students in our parent/teacher conferences;
- parents in our staff development days.

Also, as I described earlier, we learned ways to organize our staff meetings so everyone had a voice in our deliberations without adding additional time to the meetings.

Kyle: I'd love to know how to do that.

Catherine: I think that's worthy of a whole discussion by itself. Let's save organizing meetings for another day.

Before you make changes why don't you do some thinking and journaling about how you might proceed. We'll talk about your thinking and anything new you've tried next time we meet.

Kyle: I think there are few things, particularly about disseminating information, I can try right away. Resource allocation and problem solving are going to require a little more thought.

Catherine: I look forward to talking with you about your efforts and ideas when we meet next month.

Kyle: Me too. I have a lot to think about.

Conclusion

Teachers who have a sense of belonging to a larger purpose and to each other form the backbone of outstanding schools. Principals who help teachers develop a collegial culture that values and utilizes everyone's input, makes information public and widely available, and discourages in-groups and out-groups release the full energy, optimism, and collective wisdom of their faculties.

Strategies for Becoming a Reflective Leader

Journaling

Notice which teachers take advantage of your open door. Answer the following questions:

- Are they speaking only for themselves—or are they speaking for other people as well?
- Have they come to your office before?
- Is this issue they've come to discuss one that should be put on an agenda for the whole faculty to discuss?

Think about your school's current system of resource allocation.

- What are positive and negative aspects of the current system?
- How does it influence the culture of the school and the efficacy of teachers?
- How does it relate to your school's mission and goals?
- How might it be changed to better serve these needs?

Keep track of the kinds of problems you encounter in a week. Answer these questions:

- Who owns this problem? Who should be solving it?
- Is this a reoccurring problem?
- What effect does the solution to this problem have on the energy, optimism, and efficacy of the people involved?
- How does the solution to this problem affect our mission statement and goals?
- What does this problem tell us about our culture?
- How does the solution affect our culture?
- What can we learn from this problem?

Collective Wisdom/Practicing New Behaviors

Formal/Informal Communication. Work with a team (mentor, teachers) to develop a survey (using Survey Monkey or Google Forms) to uncover teachers' perceptions of ways formal and informal information flows in your school. Give the survey to the entire staff. Present results to staff and ask for feedback and suggestions. Work with mentor and team to improve the flow of information by moving as much informal information as possible to more formal venues.

Weekly Newsletter. Ask teachers to complete a short survey about the newsletter. Use the information you gather to make the newsletter more accessible and useful for teachers. Impose guidelines to keep newsletters succinct and pertinent. (e.g. number of pages, types of items) Streamline the publishing process by developing a template that a secretary can use to assemble items for the newsletter. Reserve a final edit for yourself.

Resource Allocation. Work with a mentor to develop a new plan for the allocation of resources that furthers the school's mission and goals and builds the ownership and trust that undergirds a collegial culture. Present a draft of the new plan for resource allocation to the faculty for suggestions and revisions. Put the plan into action, include a timeline for midcourse corrections and after action reviews.

Citation

1. Margaret Wheatley, *Leadership and the New Science: Learning About Organization from an Orderly Universe* (San Francisco, CA: Berrett-Koehler, 1992).

Additional Reading

Barbara Kohm and Beverly Nance, *Principals Who Learn: Asking the Right Questions Seeking the Best Solutions* (Alexandria, VA: Association for Supervision and Curriculum Development, 2007).

Linda Lambert, *Leadership Capacity for Lasting School Improvement* (Alexandria, VA: Association for Supervision and Curriculum Development, 2003).

Paul Shaw, *Taking Charge: Leading With Passion and Purpose in the Principalship* (New York, NY: Teachers College Press, 2012).

6 Making Purposeful Decisions

The Building Blocks of a Cohesive Culture

Principals are constantly making decisions. Competing interests and ambiguities make many decisions difficult. The solution to one problem can spawn a dozen more, seemingly minor decisions can become the building blocks of a new school culture, and it can feel as if a principal is drowning in minutiae. While many decisions need to be made quickly and efficiently by the principal alone, others need more deliberation and wider participation.

Principals with an awareness of how everyday decisions further or impede the core values and mission of the school provide the level of leadership that results in great schools. To become purposeful, effective decision-makers principals need:

- a framework that ties their everyday decisions to the larger purposes of the school;
- a method for discerning which decisions should be made by whom;
- a toolbox of strategies for making different kinds of decisions quickly and effectively.

In this chapter, principals and their mentors discuss ideas and tools to guide decision-making.

Developing a Framework for Purposeful Decision-Making

Principal: Jessica is a third year principal at Jefferson Elementary School
Mentor: Brad is a veteran principal from another school in Jessica's district

Jessica: We've begun to use your suggestions about ways to build teachers' learning and teaching capacity. It sounds dramatic, but it's beginning to feel like a different place around here.

Brad: How is it different?

Jessica: A new energy, optimism, and pride permeates everything we do. A feeling that was lacking or in short supply before. Folks seem eager to learn from one another and problems are addressed without the defensiveness that used to be common.

Brad: Sounds great!

Jessica: Even the conversations in the lunchroom have changed. Teachers are talking about their challenges, as well as their successes. That's new. We're still examining our beliefs about learning and how those beliefs are translated into our classrooms, and we're looking forward to our next staff development day to see how we might better align our curriculum and instruction to these beliefs.

We've gotten brave enough to discard beliefs that in the light of new learning no longer seem appropriate. We're even beginning to question the way we give grades and group students.

I asked for volunteers to help plan the next staff development day and got 15 responses—some from the very people who used to complain about having staff development days.

Now I need help making the overwhelming number of decisions I face daily. Specifically,

- deciding when to make decisions myself—and when to include other people;
- deciding when and how to make decisions quickly and effectively;
- avoiding making decisions about the same situation over and over again;

- correcting other's assumptions about my motives for making a decision;
- making difficult decisions.

It feels as if random decisions are constantly bombarding me. I'm walking down the hall; someone stops me to ask if it's okay to order extra supplies for the science fair. I get back to my office where a biology teacher has sent a student who's been disruptive in class. There's a note on my desk asking me to approve the agenda for the upcoming staff development day and another from the central office asking about plans for improving our test scores. All this happens in a ten-minute period and is repeated hundreds of times a day. It feels as if I need the wisdom of Solomon and the efficiency of a corporate CEO.

Brad: It can be daunting. I know these decisions *seem* random, but actually they are all connected … or should be. If decisions are made with a larger purpose in mind, they serve to create a culture that furthers the development of teachers, students, and the school-as-a-whole. If decisions are made randomly, they cause confusion, stagnation, and resentment. Your job is to create a unifying framework for making decisions that focuses human and material resources on previously agreed-on goals.

Jessica: We have school goals. We worked on them before school started in September. I wonder if we also need agreed-on guidelines about discipline. So many of the decisions I'm called on to make involve discipline.

Brad: Your goals and guidelines should provide a framework for the multitude of decisions you're called on to make. They should also reduce the number of decisions you need to make. For example, has your staff discussed when students should be sent to the office or when issues should be dealt with in the classroom? Or is this decision left up to each individual teacher's discretion? Is your policy based on an agreed-on philosophy of appropriate behavior and how best to teach that behavior?

At our school we hammered out an all-school discipline plan at a couple of meetings in June. We found a clearly coordinated and articulated plan that everyone on the staff, as well as parents and students, had agreed on before problems arose reduced the number of discipline problems overall and almost eliminated the number of problems sent to the principal. What started as a discipline plan focused on negative behaviors we wanted to eliminate developed into a declaration of the positive behaviors we wanted to encourage and teach.

When I needed to make a decision, it was guided by the plan we'd made together. I could send you our plan so you see what topics we covered, but you and your staff should write a policy of your own.

Jessica: Can you give me some idea of the plan you and your staff developed?

Brad: Sure. We started with the behavior we wanted to encourage rather than the infractions we thought we needed to punish. We called our plan Jefferson Students Care—about themselves, about other people, about their school and community

Under each of these headings we listed positive behaviors we wanted to develop in our students. For example, Jefferson students care about themselves so they come to class prepared; about other people so they settle conflicts with words; about their school so they don't throw trash on the floor.

We sent a draft to the PTO and the student council for their comments before we wrote a final draft. Then we sent the plan home at the start of every school year and asked parents and students to sign a sheet indicating that they had read and understood the plan.

We decided when a student should be sent to the office and when discipline would be handled in the classroom. When I spoke to students about an infraction or when I had to call a parent, I always referred to the plan. It guided my decisions and created a context teachers, students, parents, and I shared.

I have a friend who's a principal in a neighboring district. Their mission is "To inspire and prepare students as leaders, scholars, stewards, and citizens for a diverse and changing world." They use this mission statement in routine ways throughout the school. Curriculum, instruction, and discipline plans are all based on this statement. Students are recommended for commendation in each of these categories. They are also asked to write about which of these areas they violated when disciplined.

Jessica: How do you suggest we start?

Brad: You started your faculty conversations about learning by brainstorming what you believed about learning. Then you established priorities, and reviewed current teaching strategies to see how they aligned with your beliefs. I suggest you do the same with discipline.

A commonly agreed-on purpose and a plan for reaching commonly agreed-on goals will provide a framework to guide your decisions and disburse decision-making throughout your school. You'll find that decisions that once seemed random now line up to achieve a larger purpose.

Inclusive Decision-Making

Brad: Your next question was who should make which decisions. Let's start with which decisions you should make yourself and when you should include other people. My rule of thumb is to try and include as many people who will be affected by a decision as possible in the decision-making process. This means the burden of proof switches from *should someone be included* to *why shouldn't they be included.* It might mean:

- asking for input before you make a decision;
- making a decision using a simple vote or looking for consensus;
- including previously excluded groups in decision-making forums (students in parent/teacher conferences, parents in child-study meetings, or parents in staff development days).

Of course, there are always decisions that require judgment calls on the part of the principal alone. But I've found the number of these decisions is greatly reduced with good planning. Planning that provides a context in which to make decisions and a larger purpose than just the solution to an immediate problem.

Sometimes I think an issue is trivial, and make a decision that causes me to backtrack and include other people. We had a diverse population at one of my former schools. How to celebrate the winter holidays was always a problem. During his first year at our school the principal noticed the custodian put up an artificial Christmas tree in the front hall. No one seemed to pay much attention to it. He did, however get some complaints from Muslim and Jewish parents. So the next year he told the custodian not to put up the tree. It seemed like a trivial decision.

He was wrong. Some parents were very upset. From their point of view, a time-honored tradition had been violated. They even complained to the superintendent. The principal felt like the *Grinch who stole Christmas*. The following year, he formed a committee of parents from the various religious and ethnic groups that made up the school population. They worked together to develop a policy that respected everyone's beliefs. What at first seemed like a trivial decision he should just make himself became the impetus for a conversation that brought the many sectors of the school community together and laid the foundation for a more inclusive culture.

Jessica: This seems overwhelming. If nothing is trivial and I have to decide who to include in all the decisions I make every day, I'll have no time for anything else.

Brad: Actually, if you take time to plan with the folks affected by decisions, you reduce the number of decisions you need to make and the guidelines you develop make those decisions easier and less time consuming.

There are decisions that don't necessarily have a right answer but need to be made quickly and efficiently. There are others that need more deliberation and wider participation. Knowing which are which involves the art of leadership. But, you don't have to be perfect. There are always second and third chances. Notice when you find yourself making decisions about the same issues over and over again. Recurring problems are a signal that someone else needs to be included in the decision-making process or that the issue is not as trivial as you thought.

It's also important to provide clarity upfront about your decision-making process. This avoids confusion and builds trust. You might say things like:

- I plan to make a decision after we discuss the issue at our next staff meeting.
- I think this is an issue we should discuss and vote on at our next staff meeting.
- I plan to make a decision later in the week, but first I'd like to talk to everyone involved.
- I'm considering several options, but I'm not yet ready to make a decision. I think this is the kind of issue we should talk about when we plan for next year.
- I'm still undecided. I could be persuaded to go either way.

Jessica: You said there are a number of decision-making strategies you use. I'm interested in hearing about them.

Brad: Two of my favorites are *Deciding Who Pays* and *The Iceberg.*

Deciding Who Pays

Brad: My sister, an accounting professor, told me about an economic theory that helped guide many of my decisions as a principal. It's called *Who Pays?* In every transaction there is always a cost. The question is what is the cost and who pays?

When I arrived at Longview Elementary School, there was a teacher who had a biting sense of humor and frequently used sarcasm with his students. When I visited his classroom, I could see the confused and hurt look on the faces of many students when he zinged them with one of his sarcastic barbs. When I spoke to him about this, he laughed it off and said his humor was one of the things the kids really liked about him. Implying that I was a "stick in the mud." He did seem popular with some of the students and teachers who had recently elected him their union representative.

Since I was new to the school and he seemed to be one of the teacher leaders, I decided to "let it go" for the moment. I didn't want to risk making folks angry so early in my tenure. Then I began to pay attention to the cost of his humor and who was paying. I observed a few more times and confirmed my original impression. While a few favored students seemed to appreciate his humor, many more seemed confused, hurt, and silenced. I also began to pay closer attention to how he interacted with other teachers. Again a few seemed to enjoy his sarcastic barbs. Many more just stayed away. The cost in hurt feelings to individual students and teachers of his sarcasm and put-downs was higher than I originally thought.

There was also a cost to the school culture. His sarcastic put-downs had a dampening effect on conversation and exploration of new ideas among students and teachers alike. When I asked myself who was paying, the answer was the most vulnerable students and learning throughout the school. The cost was too high and the wrong people were paying.

I talked to the teacher again. This time with more conviction and made certain he understood that he would have to find another way to relate to Jefferson students and teachers. He was, as I expected, offended and said he strongly disagreed with my assessment. I offered to work with him, but made it clear there was no longer a place at Jefferson School for this kind of humor. Unfortunately, we were unable to come to an agreement and the following year he put in for a transfer. Deciding the cost of his humor and who paid gave me the clarity and courage I needed to make a decision that protected students and had a positive effect on our school's culture.

Jessica: I have a decision I've been mulling over. I wonder if deciding who pays would add clarity. About 20 percent of our students ride the buses that take them home after school. These students, all African-American, are part of a racial integration plan. Because the buses arrive before the 3:30 when school is over, we've been dismissing them at 3:20, ten minutes before other students. This cuts down on the noise and congestion in the front hall and makes dismissal run more smoothly. The teachers, bus drivers, and even I thought this was a good idea. However, when I ask myself "Who pays?" it looks different. The students who leave early miss the closing class routines everyday and are singled out as a group different from the resident students. I guess they're paying the highest price. I don't think the cost is worth the benefit, and I'm not sure the right people are paying the price. It's a decision we'll have to look at again.

Brad: A cost/benefit analysis asking who pays the cost and who gets the benefits could clarify a lot of decision-making.

I not only used this process for myself, I often used it when we needed to make a decisions as a whole staff. I'd put two columns on a flip chart. On one side we'd write the benefits of a particular course of action. On the other we'd write the costs. Then we'd go back and fill in who reaped the benefits and who paid the costs. This clarification deepened our ability to make the kind of purposeful decisions that moved our school toward our identified goals.

The Iceberg

Jessica: You mentioned having to make the same decisions over and over again. I sometimes find that happening to me.

Brad: I've found the iceberg, a systems thinking tool, valuable in this kind of situation. It helps me analyze how I may inadvertently be encouraging the very behavior I want to extinguish. I brought a model along to show you (Figure 6.1). It's such a powerful tool I knew it would eventually come up in our conversations.

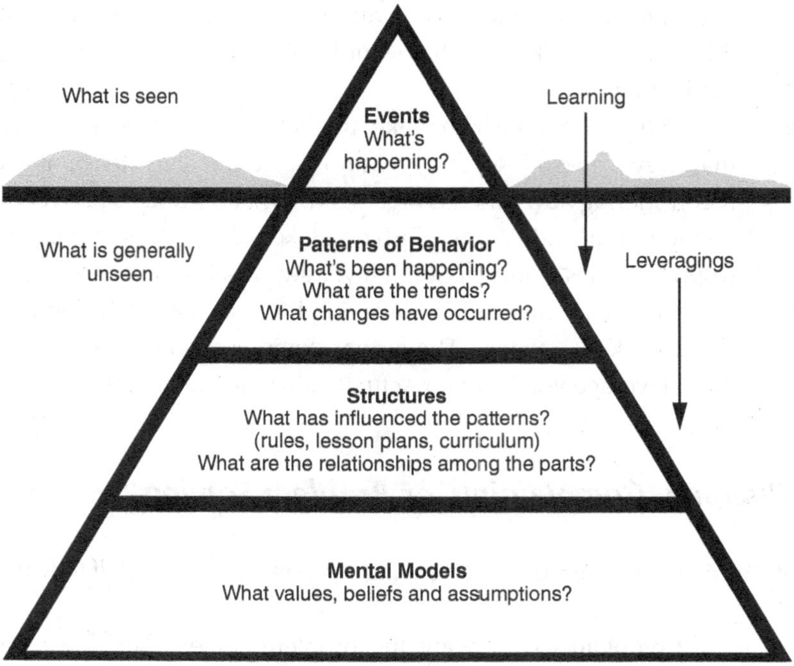

Figure 6.1 The Iceberg Model

Source: Adapted with permission from: *The Iceberg Model* by M. Goodman, 2002. (Exeter, NH: Innovation Associates Organizational Learning. Copyright ©2002 by M. Goodman.)

You start at the top of the triangle with a *concrete event*. Let's say Josh and Jake are sent to the office by the lunch monitor for fighting in the cafeteria. Then you move down to the next level and look for *patterns*. This is the third time in the past two weeks these two students have ended up in your office during lunch. It also seems as if all the students are getting louder and more boisterous during lunch. The next level is *structures*. Students have 20 minutes for lunch and 20 minutes of recess after lunch. Finally, you arrive at the bottom of the triangle, *mental models*. These are beliefs, values, and assumptions that form the basis of the rest of the structure. In this case, the belief is that we've always scheduled recess after lunch.

The analysis can be done with a large group to get to the bottom of complex problems or it can also be done quickly on your own. It's a powerful tool because it enables you to get to the root of a problem rather than just dealing with the symptoms. You mentioned dealing with the same problems over and over again. This is often a signal that you are working at the event level and need to go further down the iceberg.

In the case of Josh and Jake, the belief that "we've always done it that way" doesn't seem very strong. At the very least, it's worth reconsidering how lunch is organized. What if students had recess first and lunch second? What if Josh and Jake were given some productive responsibilities at lunch? Suddenly, new possibilities open up ... more powerful possibilities than punishing Josh and Jake that doesn't seem to be working anyway. The farther down you go on the iceberg, the more leverage you have for actually changing behavior.

Blaming, Complaining, or Problem Solving

Brad: When teachers or students bring a problem to me, I ask if they want to:

> **Complain**—They want the problem solved, but don't want to change their own behavior.
>
> **Blame**—They want someone else to change his/her behavior to solve the problem.
>
> **Problem Solve**—They are willing to change their own behavior to solve the problem.

Asking them to classify a problem in this way helps to assign responsibility and improve the efficiency of the problem-solving process. If they want to complain or blame (just blow off steam) I just listen. If they want to problem solve I work with them to make a purposeful decision.

Jessica: What if I journal about decisions I face in the next couple of weeks? I'll try to use some of the ideas we talked about today. Maybe next time we meet we can use my notes to discuss possible ways I can work with my staff to:

- develop frameworks for all of our decision-making;
- decide who should be making which decisions;
- start to collect a toolbox of decision-making strategies;
- recognize if someone wanted to blame, complain, or problem solve.

Brad: That sounds perfect. I love the way you jump in and tackle new learning situations.

Conclusion

The success of a school rests on a principal's decision-making skills. She shouldn't make every decision alone or in a vacuum. She needs to work with teachers, parents, and students to create a framework for making purposeful decisions that further the mission and goals of the school. And she needs to develop a toolbox for wise decision-making.

Becoming A Reflective Leader

Journaling

Record three or four decisions you make each day for a week. Answer the following questions:

- Did you make the decision alone or with other people?
- Did you consult with anyone else before making the decision?
- What was your decision-making process?
- What did the people affected by this decision and other community members learn about you and their community from the way you approached this decision?

- Have you worked with your school community to develop a framework for who should make this decision and how the decision might further the mission and goals of the school?
- What was the aftermath of your decision?
- If a similar situation presents itself again will you make the same decision?
- Is this a decision you've had to make before?

What do the answers to these questions tell you about your decision-making process?

What do you need to learn and do next to improve your decision-making skills and align decisions with the larger purposes of the school?

Record three decisions you've made in the past month that puzzle you. Think about the thought process you used for making those decisions.

Use the following protocols to examine each decision:

- Ask yourself "What was the price?" and "Who paid?"
- Use the "Iceberg" to analyze the underlying assumptions and structures that influenced your decision.

Would you have made a different decision if you had used these strategies to analyze the situation?

How might you use these protocols to guide future decisions?

Collective Wisdom

Work with teachers to develop frameworks for decision-making in areas that affect the whole school. Use group decision-making protocols such as brainstorming and dot voting to develop frameworks for decision-making in areas such as discipline, homework policies, goal setting, and resource allocation. Include everyone who will be affected by the decision in the process. This may involve direct decision-making or feedback on decisions someone else will make.

Learning and Teaching New Behaviors

Teach teachers about "Who Pays?' and the "Iceberg." Use them to guide group decisions.

Additional Reading

Barbara Kohm and Beverly Nance, *Principals Who Learn: Asking the Right Questions Seeking the Best Solutions* (Alexandria, VA: Association for Supervision and Curriculum Development, 2007).

Peter M. Senge et al., *Schools That Learn: A Fifth Discipline Fieldbook for Educators, Parents, and Everyone Who Cares About Education* (New York, NY: Crown Business, 2012).

7

Resolving Conflicts

Avoiding Winners and Losers

Conflict is not only inevitable—it's valuable. When hundreds of students and scores of teachers spend six hours a day, five days a week, nine months a year together on an enterprise as complex and important as education, disagreements are bound to occur. In fact if they don't, it may be a sign that there's too little passion and not enough growth or concern in your school. When you throw parents, central office personnel, and the community-at-large into that mix you have a potentially volatile stew. A volatility that can be destructive or can provide the energy and intellectual heft that moves schools forward.

In this chapter, principals and their mentors explore attitudes and protocols that untangle conflicts to reveal solutions that previously seemed impossible. They

- discuss possibilities and pitfalls of assuming good will;
- examine the difference between dialogue and discussion;
- explore three tools for analyzing conflicting points of view: 1) six points of view, 2) ladder of inference, and 3) unintended consequences;
- look at the roles risk, certainty, and ambiguity play in creating and resolving conflict.

Assuming Good Will

Principal: Shamele is the principal of a newly opened charter school
Mentor: Shawn is an old friend with many years of teaching experience

Shamele: Hi Shawn. I've been looking forward to talking with you. When the school year started, we had such an enthusiastic and positive group of teachers and parents. They were sure our charter school was the answer to their dreams.

Now they seem to be breaking into opposing camps—those who want a traditional curriculum and teaching style and those who want a more constructivist curriculum and participatory teaching style. Staff meetings have become contentious and teachers are aggravated with parents who seem to criticize everything they do. Both camps are labeling those who agree with them as *good guys* and those who oppose them as *bad guys.* They even question each other's motives saying the folks in their camp are the ones who really care about student learning. It's a situation I wanted to avoid.

Shawn: That kind of conflict can be deadly or it can provide rich learning opportunities. I suspect each side has something to learn from the other. The first thing I do when I find myself in such a conflict is to assume good will. This means assuming everyone's intentions are well meaning, even if I disagree with their conclusions or their actions.

Shamele: We're a long way from that now.

Shawn: It isn't easy. It means getting out of your own head and looking at a situation from another person's point of view. When I do this, I almost always find the other person's behavior is reasonable and often benevolent from their perspective. Even if I disagree with their assessment of a situation, I can usually acknowledge their reasonable intentions. This acknowledgment helps to open both of us up to new possibilities. If I start by assuming ill will, I almost always get pushback that shuts down possibilities for a productive resolution of the conflict.

I guess that's long way of saying, I have to change my attitude first and then help others change theirs. I think that's where you need to begin.

Shamele: What if a person actually has ill will?

Shawn: I suppose that does sometimes happen, but in my experience it's rare. I've found that most conflicts are caused by different perspectives rather than ill will. Even if you suspect ill will, I think it's worthwhile to begin with the assumption of good will. This opens a space for negotiation. Opening with an accusation almost always closes that space and makes learning and negotiation impossible.

At my present school *assume good will* has become a kind of mantra. There used to be a lot of critical talk in the teachers' lounge about parents, students, and even other teachers. Since we've been reminding ourselves to assume good will, most of that talk has faded away, leaving a space for learning.

We put some signs up around school to remind us to "assume good will" and we're even beginning to remind one another when we forget. We're also talking to students about assuming good will and plan to introduce the idea to parents at our next PTA meeting. In addition, our principal has written about assuming good will in the weekly parent newsletter. But it all started when the principal began to assume good will herself.

Shamele: That reminds me of the Gandhi quote, "Be the change you want to see in the world." I guess I'll have to begin by continually reminding myself to assume good will. You know I had a potential conflict with a parent last week that I think I handled pretty well. I didn't know to call it assuming good will, but I think that's what I did.

Shawn: Tell me about it.

Shamele: I got a call from a parent who said her child hated his teacher and hated school. She wanted me to move him to another teacher's class. I'm reluctant to do that because I'm afraid that unless there's a very good reason to honor such a request, I'll have a dozen more parents in my office requesting me to transfer their child. Even more important, I think children need to learn to work through these issues rather than being rescued by parents every time they're unhappy. In this case, the teacher was African-American and the student was white so there were potential racial issues as well. At first, I was going to talk to the parents and the teacher separately, but after I read *Leadership on the Line: Living Through the Dangers of Leading* by Heifetz and Linsky,[1] I decided to ask the teacher, parents, and student to meet with me together. The authors talked about creating a holding environment to control the heat generated by difficult situations. They said a holding environment was a space formed by a network of relationships with in which people can tackle tough issues without flying apart. I think I created a holding environment for this issue by assuming good will.

Shawn: Tell me what you did.

Shamele: I opened the meeting by asking the student what he liked about school and what he felt were his strengths. Much to everyone's surprise, he enthusiastically listed several things he liked about school. He had to think for a moment, but he was also able to list two or three of his strengths. I wrote his answers on a large flip chart. Then I turned to the teacher and asked her what she liked about the student and what she saw as his strengths. The student and his parents were surprised to hear how many positive things the teacher had to say about him. Finally, I turned to the parents and asked the same questions. The student was delighted to hear all the positive things his parents had to say about him.

I think what I was doing, although I didn't have the words at the time, was asking everyone to assume good will or, maybe more accurately, to tap in to the good will that was already there. Next I said the reason we had all come together was to solve a problem. I asked the student what that problem was. He said, "I don't like school. It's not as much fun as last year." I wrote what the student said on the chart and asked the teacher and parents to add anything they thought would clarify the problem. Finally, I said we needed to use all the strengths we'd listed to help solve the problem. The good will created by the first exercise created a space for solving the problem.

The mother reported that every day when her son came home from school she asked how his school day had been. Almost everyday he reported something negative that happened at school and they would have a conversation about the negative event. I suspected his mother was unintentionally encouraging a focus on the few things he felt went wrong rather than the many things that went right in his day. We decided to refocus the student's attention by asking him to write three good things that happened at school to report to his mother in addition to whatever else he wanted to report. I gave the parents the chart paper with all the good things written on it and we agreed to check with one another in a week to see how things are going. After the first week, student and parents reported things had improved greatly. We hadn't addressed any of the student's original complaints. Instead we broadened the context to include all the many good things that happened every day. That seemed to solve the problem. After three weeks, the positive notes weren't needed any more. I think that by assuming good will we created a space that avoided conflict and allowed a carefully targeted solution to emerge.

I knew that at rock bottom everyone wanted the student to have a good school experience. In this case, a refocus rather than lots of problem solving which would have kept the student focused on what he perceived as negative events seemed to be the ticket. After a while, the mom said her son reported on a full range of activities when he came home from school. The negative focus melted away even though his class placement hadn't changed.

Shawn: That's terrific! I'm going to use this method myself. You started by assuming good will. Some folks might have been uneasy about having everyone in the room at the same time, but that proved to be the key to your success. That and focusing on the good will in the room before tackling the problems.

Dialogue Versus Discussion

Principal: Kyle is the new principal of Oakville Middle School
Mentor: Catherine is a retired principal assigned to Kyle as a mentor

Kyle: We've been talking about including students in our parent teacher conferences and parents in our student staffings. One group of teachers is all gung ho about the idea. Another group says, "Wait a minute, we're not so sure that's a good idea." The first group says there's more leverage in talking *with* people than *about* them. The second group says they would feel inhibited discussing sensitive issues if both students and parents were at these meetings. I could issue an edict, but I think that would just drive the issue underground. Do you have any suggestions?

Catherine: I think it might be a good idea to talk about resolving conflicts in general. A good place to start might be the difference between dialogue and discussion. Our assistant superintendent introduced the concept to us several years ago. It's helped us learn from conflicts rather than shying away from them. We make better decisions and our decision-making process no longer leaves a residue of resentment and hurt feelings. Basically the idea is simple.

- The purpose of dialogue is to understand other people's points of view.
- The purpose of discussion is to make a decision.

Separating and labeling two different kinds of conversations has been enormously helpful. When we're faced with a conflict, we often set aside the first part of a meeting for dialogue and the second part for discussion. If there's room, we make two circles and sit in one for dialogue and one for discussion to emphasize the difference in the two processes.

During *dialogue,* participants refrain from defending their own ideas or contradicting others' opinions and concentrate instead on understanding other people's points of view. This means asking more questions and making fewer statements.

During *discussion,* each side advocates for their position. We often vote or use a consensus protocol to conclude the meeting. I'm on the committee that negotiates with the teachers' organizations about salary. Our deliberations have changed 100 percent since we've been separating *dialogue* and *discussion.*

I don't suppose everyone's always happy with our decisions, but they know where the other side is coming from and why the decision was made. This enables us to hold together as a community instead of fragmenting into isolated groups.

Kyle: That sounds interesting and powerful. I think it might be helpful in resolving our issues about who to include in various kinds of conversations. Before we schedule a meeting, I'd like to give my leadership team or maybe even the entire staff something to read about dialogue and discussion. Is there anything you'd suggest?

Catherine: There's book by the physicist, David Bohm called *On Dialogue.*[2] In it there's a chapter called "Designing a Dialogue Session" by William Isaacs and Bryan Smith (pp. 374–381). I'd also look at *The Fifth Discipline Fieldbook* by Peter Senge.[3]

Tools for Analyzing Conflicts

Principal: Jessica is a third year principal at Jefferson Elementary School
Mentor: Brad is a veteran principal from another school in her district

Six Points of View

Jessica: A disagreement has erupted on our staff about field trips. Some teachers feel a student needs to earn the privilege of going on a field trip by doing her work and behaving properly. Other teachers argue that this results in our most vulnerable students being left behind and missing important learning experiences. As a result, different teachers have different standards. This is confusing for students and parents. The confusion often ends up in my office in the form of angry students, teachers, and parents.

Brad: I learned a clever and powerful strategy at a systems thinking conference a few years ago. It's helped our staff get a handle on this kind of conflict. It's called "Six Points of View." Like many of these systems thinking strategies, it's simple and profound at the same time.

You assign six different people to represent six different points of view. In your case, you might have a teacher from the group that believes students need to earn the privilege of going on field trips, a teacher who believes all students should go on field trips, a student who always goes on field trips, a student who gets left behind, a parent whose child always behaves well, and a parent of a child who gets left behind. That's six points of view. Next have each person talk about the situation from his or her perspective.

This in itself won't resolve the conflict, but it will provide a space for everyone to examine the problem from various perspectives before making a decision. My experience has been that after hearing everyone's viewpoint, most groups come up with a solution they hadn't thought of before. A solution that includes elements from many perspectives and a solution they can all agree on.

Jessica: You mean we might be able to find a middle ground where one seemed impossible before?

Brad: It could be that, but more often groups come up with something entirely new. Something no one had thought of before.

Jessica: I'm thinking we may need two staff meetings for this exercise—one to role play six points of view, with time to think about what we learned, and another to establish a policy.

Brad: Sounds perfect. One other thing, I not only use this strategy with my faculty, I also use it with myself when I'm getting into an adversarial situation with someone. Forcing myself to see at least two or three other points of view stretches my thinking and opens up a space for creative problem solving.

Jessica: It might be particularly useful when I start feeling self-righteous. I know self-righteousness is dangerous, but it feels so good to be so right I sometimes find it hard to let go of that certainty.

Brad: Six Points of View is good for that, but I have a strategy that may be even better. It's called the Ladder of Inference (Figure 7.1).

Ladder of Inference

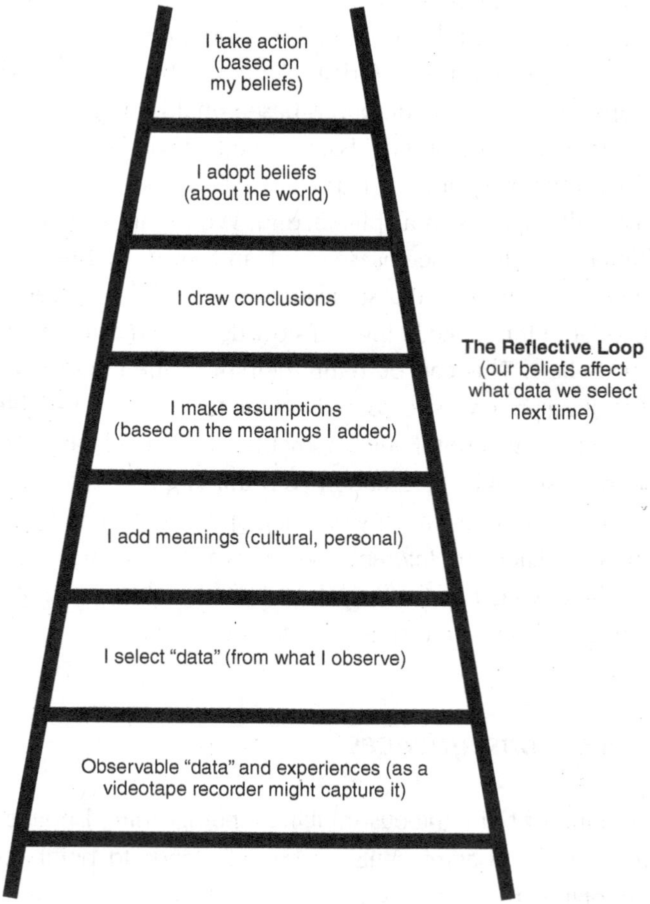

Figure 7.1 The Ladder of Inference

Source: Adapted from: Peter M. Senge, *The Fifth Discipline: The Art and Practice of The Learning Organization* (New York, NY: Doubleday/Currency, 1990).

Brad: It works likes this. At the bottom of the ladder is some observable data. In your case it might be that a particular teacher has left several students at school when she took her class on a field trip. Next, you select one piece of data to focus on and season it with your own cultural and personal biases. You notice that most of the students left behind are African-American boys. You conclude this teacher doesn't know how to teach African-American boys or maybe she doesn't understand or even like them. Then you make assumptions based on your observations and the meanings you've assigned to them. White female teachers can't understand or effectively teach African-American boys. Finally you adopt beliefs about the world based on your assumptions and take actions based on your beliefs. On the other hand, you might conclude from your observations that African-American boys cause problems on field trips. Then make assumptions based on this observation. In either case, you veer off the original issue of students on field trips and begin to discuss the behavior of African-American boys.

This all happens in a split second. We're rarely even aware that it's happening. It all seems so right and easy. In the process you inadvertently reinforce the same erroneous thinking over and over. The Ladder of Inference helps you slow down and examine the source of your beliefs. This can be really helpful in the middle of a heated conflict. It's a great way to counteract the feelings of self-righteousness you were talking about. Feelings, by the way, we all have. The trick is to use these strategies to broaden your thinking.

Jessica: Do you have an extra copy of that graphic? I'd like to keep it on my desk until the Ladder of Inference becomes a routine part of my thinking. It might help me get off that high horse of self-righteous thinking.

Brad: You might also want to share it with your staff.

Unintended Consequences

Jessica: Speaking of self-righteous thinking, another thing I notice happens when we have disagreements—each side tends to point out all the benefits of their point of view and to ignore the possible pitfalls. I think in our zeal to convince other people of our point of view, we have blinders about the possible unintended consequences of our own proposals.

Brad: That's the reason you need a loyal opposition. It's by listening to opposing points of view that we make better decisions. We often have blinders on, particularly when we're zealous about our ideas. We need someone to slow us down and help us examine the possible consequences of our plans. That's the value of conflict. The trick is to find a strategy that provides a neutral space for predicting what these consequences might be. That can't happen when everyone is spending all their energies defending their own positions.

Jessica: How do you do that?

Brad: We've already talked about *Six Points of View* and the *Ladder of Inference*. Let's see if we can come up with a strategy for predicting unintended consequences.

Jessica: What about using a *T-chart* to record all the consequences, positive and negative that might result from leaving kids at school who don't earn the field trip or allowing everyone to go on the field trips. We'd have two flip charts, one for each point of view. On each chart we'd list possible positive consequences on one side of the chart and possible negative consequences on the other.

Brad: That sounds great. You're beginning to get the hang of collaborative leadership. My guess is that a new solution no one thought of before will emerge from this process.

Certainty, Risk, and Tolerance for Ambiguity

Principal: Kyle is the new principal of Oakville Middle School
Mentor: Catherine is a retired principal assigned to Kyle as a mentor

Kyle: I've been working with teachers on the difference between dialogue and discussion. It's definitely helped, but it's more difficult than it sounded when we talked.

Some folks are absolutely certain they know what's best for children. They've developed their beliefs over a long teaching career. One teacher asked me, "Are you saying everything I've been doing for the past twenty years is wrong?" It's not easy to ask teachers to give up or even question the certainties on which they've built their practice. I told her, "Of course not, we stand on your shoulders, but we need to keep learning, growing, and responding to changing circumstances."

Catherine: You're asking them to move from certainty to ambiguity. That's difficult, but essential for growth. If you want to create a healthy learning culture, one that uses conflict as a springboard to creativity and is continually improving, you have to deal with issues of uncertainty, ambiguity, and risk.

Kyle: How do you do that?

Catherine: By doing all the things we've already talked about and doing them over and over again. You have to create a psychological space where creative thinking can flourish.

It begins by assuming good will. Giving up certainty and dealing with ambiguity and risk are scary. Folks aren't likely to risk the safety of the status quo, if they feel their character and motives are being attacked. They're more likely to come out swinging and break into like-minded camps that talk behind each other's backs.

You have to establish a theory of learning for teachers and students that includes learning from mistakes, changing course when new information is available, and detaching ego from opinions.

Kyle: That's a lot to think about.

Catherine: I know. It helps to summarize:

- In every conflict, there's a kernel of opportunity.
- Changing your mind is not a sign of weakness. It's called learning.
- Focus on the content of the conflict, not the people.
- Don't be afraid of conflict. Positive energy and good ideas are buried there.

Instead of winners and losers, create a culture of learners.

Conclusion

Conflict is not only inevitable, but if handled well, it's also valuable. Skillful principals develop holding environments where creative thinking and successful solutions can emerge from the thinking and passion of opponents. These leaders assume good will and use tools such as *Dialogue and Discussion, Six Points of View, Ladder of Inference,* and *T-charts* of Unintended Consequences to create these holding environments. They also deal directly with the uncertainty, ambiguity, and risk that accompany change by establishing a theory of learning for teachers and students that includes learning from mistakes, changing course when new information is available, and detaching ego from opinions.

Strategies for Becoming a Reflective Leader

Journaling

Think about two or three conflicts you have dealt with in the past or are currently dealing with. How might you use the assumption of good will, agreement on intentions, and examination of different perspectives to create a safe holding environment where creative thinking and successful solutions can emerge?

Collective Wisdom

Help teachers develop a collective theory of learning and continual improvement that includes learning from mistakes, changing course when new information becomes available, and detaching ego from opinions. The conversation might begin with a brainstorming session of beliefs about learning and continue with conversations throughout the year. These conversations might focus on analyzing new situations in light of current beliefs—and altering those beliefs as the team's collective wisdom grows.

Use tools such as *Six Points of View, Ladder of Inference,* and *T-charts* to aid in decision-making and to broaden and deepen thinking.

Discuss uncertainty, ambiguity, and risk directly and honestly as normal and necessary elements of growth and change.

Practicing New Behaviors

When conflicts arise, develop safe holding environments by assuming good will and focusing on intentions. Use your journal and conversations with your mentor to analyze the success of these endeavors to improve your skills.

Begin to view conflict as a source of creative thinking and uncertainty, ambiguity, and risk as normal elements of learning and growth.

Citations

1. Ronald A. Heifetz and Marty Linsky, *Leadership on the Line: Living Through the Dangers of Leading* (Boston, MA: Harvard Business School Publishing, 2002).
2. David Bohm, *On Dialogue* (New York, NY: Routledge, 1996).
3. Peter M. Senge, *The Fifth Discipline Fieldbook: Strategies and Tools for Building a Learning Organization* (New York, NY: Doubleday, 1999).

Additional Reading

Sharon A. Brunink, *Lessons from My Inner Teacher: Intuitive Journaling as a Tool For Growth* (Bloomington, IN: Balboa Press, 2013).

Peter Senge et al., *Schools That Learn: A Fifth Discipline Fieldbook for Educators, Parents, and Everyone Who Cares About Education* (New York, NY: Doubleday, 2000).

8 Planning Meetings

Learning and Leading Together

Meetings can be a deadly waste of time or the lynch pin that enables a faculty to learn and grow together. In this chapter, principals and their mentors craft meetings that stimulate creative problem solving, tap into the collective wisdom of the entire faculty, and improve everyone's classroom practice. Meetings in which e-mail and phone distractions are eliminated and everyone is fully engaged. Principals and their mentors discuss the following ways to organize such meetings:

- have a clear purpose for each meeting;
- meet regularly;
- arrange seating;
- set a tone;
- establish norms;
- provide time for quiet reflection;
- get every voice in the air;
- develop effective and efficient agendas;
- make group decisions;
- value conflict.

Having a Clear Purpose for Each Meeting and Meet Regularly

Principal: Shamele is the principal of a newly opened charter school
Mentor: Shawn is an old friend with many years of teaching experience

Shamele: Many teachers are feeling overwhelmed and are beginning to complain about coming to meetings. That puts me in a bind. I'm sympathetic with their frustration, but I know we can't make group decisions or learn together unless we get together on a regular basis.

Shawn: We had the same problem at our school. The better we got, the more we needed to meet. The more we met the greater the time-crunch and pushback. It's what you call a Catch-22.

Shamele: What did you do?

Shawn: We decided as a faculty to have shorter, more frequent, and more focused meetings. We decided to hold weekly meetings for 45 minutes before school. That way we were forced to end on time and make more efficient use of our time together. We decided that at least 30 minutes would be for learning or discussion that directly affected student learning. We use a timed agenda to discipline ourselves and the principal takes responsibility for starting and ending the meeting on time and sticking to the agenda.

Shamele: What if there's nothing to discuss?

Shawn: There's always something to learn or discuss in a school where everyone is working to continually improve their practice. Every spring, after our faculty finishes writing annual goals, we develop a timeline for the coming school year that includes a list of discussion topics for our staff meetings. We align these topics with the school year and the school goals we have just created. This long-term planning keeps us from filling our agendas with last minute topics unrelated to our school goals and ensures there is always a clear purpose for each meeting. We put butcher paper on a long wall; draw a month-by-month calendar for the school year. We then use sticky notes to indicate when various activities—including meetings and discussion topics—will take place. The calendar gives us a visual picture of the whole year, and the sticky notes make it possible to move events around to create a manageable and reasonable flow to the year. Before we created this long-range look, we were continually using meetings to react to problems rather than to prevent them.

I've worked in schools where the faculty met infrequently and waited until the last minute to write agendas for staff meetings. These schools lacked the coherent, collaborative spirit and focus on continual improvement that our school has achieved. I think if a faculty, department, or grade level team meets infrequently, they lose the energy and drive that coherence provides.

Arranging Seating

Shamele: We hold our staff meetings in the library where teachers sit at tables of four to six people. Mostly they sit with and talk to the same people, folks with whom they're most familiar and comfortable. There are a lot of side conversations and little sense of the faculty as a whole.

Shawn: We've experimented with different seating arrangements for our staff meetings. I've been amazed at how much difference such a detail makes. We'd always met in our library as well. When the library was being renovated we were forced to move to the music room where the only way we could all fit in was to sit in a circle. It took only a few meetings for us to realize how different our meetings were when we sat in a different configuration. The principal was no longer in the front and the focus of our conversations. We spoke directly to one another, built on each other's ideas, and gave constructive feedback. We are all more exposed and more engaged than we'd been at library tables. In a circle, everyone can see and speak directly to every one else. And since everyone is visible, it minimizes side conversation and eliminates phone distractions.

Shamele: I get it! Planning good meetings is just like planning good lessons. Details like seating arrangements that seem inconsequential can make a big difference in how people interact and learn from one another.

Shawn: In fact circle-seating arrangements have a long history of promoting discourse. Native Americans and academics have long used seminar circles to promote dynamic discussions. Easy eye contact and egalitarian seating enable all voices to be heard and valued.

Establishing Norms

Shawn: The other thing we did that made a difference was establishing norms. I suppose, either consciously or unconsciously, every group develops norms about how they'll be together. The trick is to make them intentional and explicit.

Shamele: In my experience, norms often go the way of mission statements. They are someone else's ideas, seldom referred to, and never used to actually guide behavior.

Shawn: I think it's your job as principal to work with your faculty to develop norms and make certain they guide your work together. If one of your norms is "No side conversations," you need to remind folks who are talking to the person next to them during a group conversation to address their comments to the whole group.

A common and useful norm is "No parking lot conversations." This means discussing important issues with the whole faculty at regularly scheduled staff meetings rather than with a few like-minded colleagues in the parking lot after the meeting. This norm is harder to enforce but important. It brings everyone's thinking to bear on important issues and prevents the balkanization of a faculty.

Shamele: Calling people out who violate those norms could be awkward.

Shawn: It could be. But once the faculty sets norms for their work together, it's your responsibility to make sure they're adhered to.

Shamele: I've been to workshops where we set norms for our time together. Would it be okay to use one of those lists?

Shawn: Put those lists in your back pocket in case you need them, but I think it's better if each group writes their own norms. This forces a conversation that ensures clarity and commitment to the norms. It might be useful to start with "No side conversations" or "No parking lot conversations" to get things started. Usually, the conversation flows after that. If not, use those lists in your back pocket to stimulate more ideas.

Setting a Tone

Shamele: I want our meetings to be serious and focused. At the same time, I'd like to find a way to infuse a sense of fun, energy, and optimism in them.

Shawn: A few months ago, our principal went to a systems thinking conference. She said as you came into each session there was music playing. She's been trying the same thing with our staff meetings. She has the music teacher select a CD to play as we walk into a meeting. It creates a quiet, relaxed, and attentive mood. I wonder if music might infuse your meetings and your faculty with the focused energy and optimism you want.

Shamele: I love the idea! Next time we meet, I'll give it a try and let you know how it goes.

Providing Time for Quiet Reflection

Shawn: You may also want to provide time for quiet reflection. Teachers' lives are hectic. Students, parents, and administrators are constantly making demands on their time. Time for quiet reflection is in short supply. Providing a few minutes of quiet for teachers to gather their thoughts before a dialogue or discussion is welcome and useful. Teachers, like students, have different learning and communication styles. Some folks have ideas on the tips of their tongues. They're ready with an answer or a suggestion the minute a question is asked or a topic proposed. Others need time to organize their thoughts. A few minutes of quiet time to think through what they want to say and jot down a few notes enables them to fully participate in the conversation. These folks are often deep thinkers who have valuable ideas to share.

Shamele: I'm not sure how to make that happen.

Shawn: First, you have to build reflection time into the agenda - say five minutes before discussing an important topic. When we first started building time for reflection in our agendas, it took a while for everyone to quiet down. But it wasn't long before everyone began to value this time and focus immediately.

Shamele: I'm in the process of writing our next staff meeting agenda. I think I'll give five minutes of quiet reflection a try.

Getting Every Voice in the Air

Shawn: Another change I've noticed in our staff meetings is that everyone participates. That didn't used to happen. Before, only a few people talked and the rest of us listened or, more likely, tuned out. We lost too many voices.

Shamele: Why do more people speak up now?

Shawn: Many reasons. We've already talked about a few—sitting in a circle, having a voice in how meetings are structured, establishing norms, and using some systems thinking tools. One tool is "getting every voice in the air" early in a meeting. Something kind of magic happens when folks speak early in a meeting. They feel more engaged and present. The opposite happens when they are silent. It's easy to disengage and let someone else speak for you. This means if you want a fully engaged faculty, you need to provide an opportunity for every voice to be heard early in the meeting. Round robin discussions are a good way to begin.

Round Robin Discussions. The principal or discussion leader poses a question and asks everyone to weigh in with an answer. A question might be what's one thing you've tried with a struggling student? Or what's an activity you've planned for math curriculum night to help parents better understand our new math program? Ask teachers to answer the question in two or three sentences. One can pass if she doesn't want to answer the question. It's a quick and easy way to tap into and expand the collective wisdom of the group.

Developing Effective and Efficient Agendas

Shamele: I get it! Staff meetings are my classroom and I need to be as purposeful and attentive to details in planning those meetings as I expect teachers to be in planning lessons.

Shawn: Right! Teachers are busy people. The principals I've known who are respectful of teachers' time and understand the value of group learning and decision-making spend time carefully constructing agendas. These are their lesson plans. They review agendas to make certain:

- They are timed. The time allotted to each subject is realistic, efficient, and public (written on the agenda). This gives participants the information they need to curb or focus their comments.
- There is an opportunity early in the meeting to get every voice in the air.
- There is a clear focus for the meeting.
- Announcements are dealt with by e-mail or other means.
- Discussions are kept focused and to the point.
- Tools and protocols are used to make effective and efficient use of time.
- There is time for quiet reflection.

Shamele: I've tried doing timed agendas, but I find it hard to know exactly how much time each item will take.

Shawn: It's a learned skill. You'll get better with time.

Shamele: What about beginning and ending meetings on time. I always have a few stragglers and we're not always finished at the allotted time.

Shawn: That's a problem with every group that meets regularly. You have the responsibility to teach folks to respect the beginning and ending times of meetings.

Shamele: I'm not sure I know what you mean.

Shawn: I always start meetings at the exact time I say I will, even if there are only a few people present. When others arrive, I just continue on. Once in a while, I'll acknowledge their presence, but usually not. Over time, folks get the message that meetings will start exactly on time. If I wait five or ten minutes for everyone to show up, many folks will begin to show up five or ten minutes later. I've made it worse and wasted the time of the folks who showed up on time. I've found I don't need to admonish people for being late. If I just consistently start on time, the problem solves itself.

Shamele: What about ending on time, especially if I haven't covered all the items on the agenda?

Shawn: The first thing is to remain aware of the time when you're running a meeting. If you're in the middle of a meeting and realize you won't make it through the whole agenda, you can do one of several things:

- Save an item or two for the next meeting.
- Rearrange the order of items and make other arrangements for the last items. You might put the item on e-mail or on a poster in the teachers' lounge and ask for written feedback or other comments. You might also decide to just drop an item that doesn't seem so important any more.
- Cut a discussion short and move on to the next item. Ask for follow up comments on e-mail or put the item on a future agenda.

Shamele: What about folks who just go on and on, who have already made their point and given several examples. I think some people just like to hear themselves talk, and others can't seem to draw an idea to a conclusion.

Shawn: I know that's awkward, but it's your job to keep the conversation focused and everyone engaged. That means making time and space for more than a few voices. Google conducted research on the effectiveness of teams and concluded the following: "As long as everyone got a chance to talk, the team did well. But if only one person or a small group spoke all the time, the collective intelligence declined."

It helps to refer to the time limit on the agenda and redirect the speaker. "We've only allotted 15 minutes for this topic, and I want to make sure we finish the agenda. Would you please put their thoughts in writing for the next staff memo, or e-mail them to everyone?"

Shamele: I'd like to go over our next staff meeting agenda with you. I'd also like to talk more about systems thinking tools that enable teachers to make collaborative decisions in a timely manner.

Making Group Decisions

Shamele: As you suggested, I've been trying to move from an open door to an open school. I know that means talking to the faculty as a whole whenever I can rather than just speaking to the folks who ask for individual conferences. But this has created a new problem. We only have scheduled staff meetings every other week for an hour and a half. We hardly have time to get through the business we need to discuss, much less try to collectively solve problems.

Shawn: I know that's tough and you certainly don't want to call any more meetings or make them any longer. I went to a conference last year and learned some System Thinking Tools that have made our meetings much more efficient and productive. I've also learned a lot from reading *The Adaptive School.*[1] I have a copy on my shelf. I'd be glad to lend you, but I think it would be worth your while to invest in a copy yourself.

Shamele: I'll do that. In the mean time, can you get me started? We have a meeting on Monday and I'd love to give one of those tools a try.

Shawn: Here are three tools I find I use most often.

Brainstorming and Dot Voting are good for making group decisions and setting priorities. The discussion leader poses a question or problem that needs a solution. The group brainstorms possible solutions to the problem. The rules are simple: 1) all solutions no matter how seemingly far-fetched are accepted, and 2) all solutions are recorded on a surface (flip chart, dry erase board, or screen) that everyone can see. There is no discussion of individual solutions except for clarification by the recorder during the brainstorming process. After all the ideas are recorded, group members can ask for clarification or explanation. The idea is that criticism at early stages in the process can stifle creativity. Even seemingly outlandish ideas can stimulate thinking and lead to a solution no one thought of before.

After the brainstorm list is complete, each participant is given two or three sticky dots and asked to put them on the two or three solutions they think are best. When everyone has placed his/her dots on the chart a visual picture of the group's thinking emerges. This is the kind of clarity that never happens when teachers only speak to few like-minded friends or the principal only talks to those people who take advantage of her open door policy. Once priorities are established and visually expressed, group decisions are more easily and efficiently made.

The Iceberg is good for issues that need more in-depth analysis (Figure 8.1).

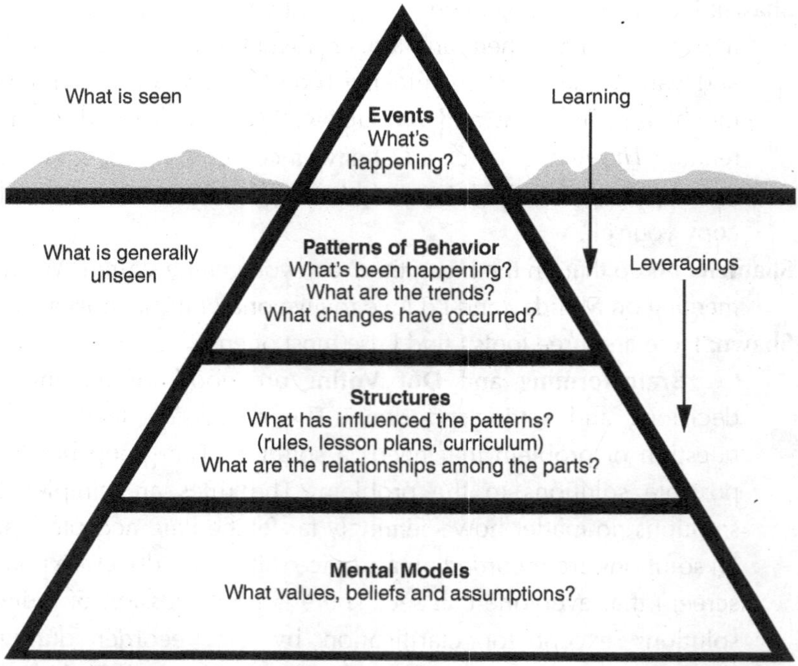

Figure 8.1 The Iceberg Model
Source: Adapted with permission from: *The Iceberg Model* by M. Goodman, 2002. (Exeter, NH: Innovation Associates Organizational Learning. Copyright ©2002 by M. Goodman.)

You start at the top of the triangle with an observation or concrete event.

- Antoine, a fourth grade student, is sent to your office for disruptive behavior in math class.
- Then you move down to the next level and look for patterns. *This is the third time in the past two weeks Antoine has been sent your office.* He had no previous referrals.
- Moving down the model to systems that are in place that might be affecting this situation. *The teacher has recently divided students into ability groups for math instruction and Antoine is in the lowest group.*
- Finally, you arrive at the bottom of the triangle, mental models. These are beliefs, values, and assumptions that form the basis of the rest of the structure. *Some students are more capable of learning math than other students and each group is best taught with students of similar ability.*

This analysis can help a large group think through an issue and to get to the bottom of complex problems in a short time. Is the belief at the bottom of the triangle still valid? What if we change that belief or experiment with a different theory? How might that change our systems, patterns, and student learning and behavior? It's a powerful tool because it enables a group to get to the root of a problem rather than just dealing with the symptoms. When a group is dealing with the same problems over and over again, it's often a signal they are working at the event level and need to go further down the iceberg to really solve the problem.

Shamele: Once you've done this analysis, is a straightforward vote the best way to make group decisions?

Shawn: It depends on what you want. I think it's important to be clear with everyone up front about who will make a decision and how it will be made. You might want to:

- make the decision yourself once you have information about the groups thinking gleaned;
- decide with a simple vote from the faculty;
- discuss the issue until you reach consensus from the whole group.

It's important to describe what your decision-making process will be up front. Then put any decisions the faculty makes in writing and distribute them after the meeting. This creates a written common understanding of what was decided. I'm always surprised at what different interpretations folks have of group decisions. Putting the decision in writing creates an opportunity to clear up any misunderstandings.

If you think the problem needs further analysis systems thinking tools such as Six Points of View and the Ladder of Inference might be helpful.

Six Points of View helps a group analyze an issue from six different points of view. A new math program might be examined from the point of view of a student who struggles in math, a student who's a math whiz, a new teacher, a veteran teacher, a curriculum director, and a parent of a student who struggles in math. Staff members can role-play or simply reflect on these viewpoints to get a broader understanding of the issue.

Ladder of Inference is a tool that helps uncover unconscious thinking about an issue (Figure 8.2). You start at the bottom of the ladder with *observable data* (Josh has failed to turn in his math homework for the past two weeks), then very quickly, usually without realizing it, you *select particular data* (Josh never turns in math homework.), you then make *assumptions* about Josh (he's irresponsible, unwilling to work hard, and not good at math, comes from a home where there's little support). Next you draw conclusions based on your assumptions (Josh needs to be moved to a less demanding math class); the assumption is based on the belief that struggling students do better in less demanding classes with other struggling students. Finally, you take action and move Josh to a lower math group.

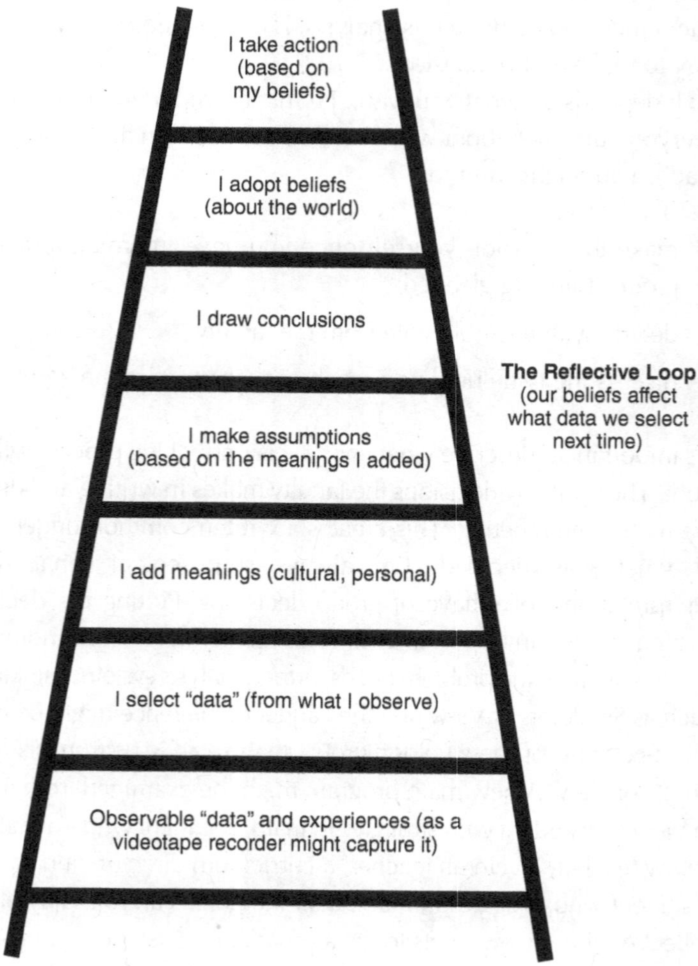

Figure 8.2 The Ladder of Inference

Source: Adapted from: Peter M. Senge, *The Fifth Discipline: The Art and Practice of The Learning Organization* (New York, NY: Doubleday/Currency, 1990).

Because this thought process is mostly unconscious, it's difficult to correct it. The Ladder of Inference provides a tool to help uncover the thoughts and believes that undergird our decisions.

Valuing Conflict

Shamele: When our meetings mostly consisted of announcements and presentations, we rarely had to deal with conflict. Now that we're discussing issues that really matter to people, we're having more disagreements.

Shawn: That's actually a sign of growth. When everyone is encouraged to express their feelings and ideas, you get the benefit of everyone's thinking and some inevitable disagreements. When conflicts are discouraged, teachers lose opportunities to learn from one another.

Shamele: We have little experience with face-to-face confrontations. Unless we learn how to handle conflict better, I'm afraid we'll just stay in our comfortable cliques where we massage each others' egos and little learning takes place.

Shawn: What we did was first to say out loud what was going on. We were having more conflicts because we were growing. Next, we made some agreements with one another about how we would behave when we had conflicts. We decided to:

- disagree with someone's ideas without discrediting that person;
- be clearer and more specific in our thinking and communication;
- stop labeling people and assuming we know what they were thinking before they speak;
- listen fully and carefully to everyone, particularly those who disagree with us.

Living up to these commitments was extraordinarily difficult. Time and again when we felt attacked personally or unsure of our own position, we reverted to name-calling and parking lot conversations. Some of us became bullies. Others failed to stand up for principles they believed in. However, by returning to the commitments we'd made to one another, using the consensus building tools we were learning, and not backing away from difficult discussions, we gradually learned to value conflict and grow together.

It's now okay to throw out a half-baked idea with the expectation that the group will help think it through. This may include poking holes in your thinking. But it doesn't mean disparaging you as a person. Each of us is now smarter than any of us would be alone. The constructive clash of ideas has enabled us to raise our standards for student work and improve our teaching skills.

Shamele: What were the consensus building skills you were learning?

Shawn: Probably the most useful was learning to make a distinction between discussion and dialogue.

Shamele: What is the difference? I think I use them interchangeably.

Shawn: The purpose of dialogue is to understand another person's point of view. The purpose of discussion is to convince some else of your point of view. They each have a place in your staff meetings, but it's important to distinguish between the two.

We begin our consensus building with dialogue. The questions we asked were designed to gain a deeper understanding of someone else's thinking, not to present opposing points of view. Those had to wait for the discussion phase of the consensus building process.

Because the rules of dialogue forced us to listen carefully to one another's thinking, we developed a deeper understanding of complexity. And because we wanted our colleagues to understand us, we learned to be clearer and more precise in our explanations. As a result, we're now less likely to look for simple one-time solutions to complex problems.

I have a friend who uses dialogue with her staff. They form two circles, one for dialogue and one for discussion, and move back and forth depending on the purpose of the conversation. She says this helps them establish and stay in the mindset of either dialogue or discussion.

Shamele: This conversation has given me a great deal to think about.

Shawn: One more thing ... we've talked about a lot of ways to make your meetings more efficient, participatory, and productive. But I think the most important take-away from our conversation today is that successful meetings are a crucial part of successful schools. And successful meetings need to be as carefully and skillfully planned as successful lessons.

Conclusion

Meetings: a deadly waste of time or the life-blood of a fully functioning, collaborative faculty? It's a principal's job to put into place the structures and cultural underpinnings that result in the kind of vibrant meetings that give rise to a culture clearly focused on mutually agreed-on goals, responsive to changing circumstances, and committed to continual improvement.

Strategies for Becoming a Reflective Leader

Journaling

After the next three staff meetings, answer these questions:

- Did the meetings begin and end on time?
- Did you follow the agenda as written? What adjustments might have made it more focused and realistic? Were the time allotments realistic? Did you have sufficient time for the most important items? Did you distribute the agenda before the meeting?
- How many people were active participants in the conversation? Were there any or many people who were only passive receivers of information?
- Was there an opportunity to "get every voice in the air" early in the meeting?
- Was there time for quiet reflection?
- What was accomplished?
- What items could have been dealt with in some other way? (e.g. weekly memo)
- What items didn't you get to?
- How did the seating arrangement affect the quality of the meeting? (Discourage side conversations, enable teachers to speak directly to one another, encourage the active participation of all group members.)

Collective Wisdom

Periodically survey teachers about their responses to the staff meeting format and agenda. Ask for suggestions for improvement.

Change Behavior

Work with teachers to establish norms for meetings. Make certain norms are adhered to and periodically reviewed.

Incorporate "The Iceberg," "Six Points of View," and "Ladder of Inference" into faculty discussions in order to mine the ideas hidden in conflict.

Citation

1. Robert Garmston and Bruce Wellman, *The Adaptive School: A Sourcebook for Developing Collaborative Groups* (Lanham, MD: Roman and Littlefield, 2016).

Additional Reading

Barbara Kohm and Beverly Nance, *Principals Who Learn: Asking the Right Questions Seeking the Best Solutions* (Alexandria, VA: Association for Supervision and Curriculum Development, 2007).

Peter M. Senge, *Schools That Learn: A Fifth Discipline Fieldbook for Educators, Parents, and Everyone Who Cares About Education* (New York, NY: Crown Business, 2012).

Dannelle D. Stevens and Joanne E. Cooper, *Journal Keeping: How to Use Reflective Writing for Learning, Teaching, Professional Insight and Positive Change* (Sterling, VA: Stylus Publishing LLC, 2009).

9 Collecting and Using Data

What Story Does Your Data Tell?

Schools are awash in anecdotes and long-held beliefs that may or may not be true. Data can clarify what's really happening. Are there certain math concepts students fail to grasp year after year? Is discipline a problem in the halls, but not in the classrooms? Are some student groups falling behind others? Successful principals work with teachers to collect and use data to tell the story of what children are learning, pinpoint effective ways to improve instruction, and motivate students to persist to mastery. The science of data collection married to the art of teaching results in great teaching and outstanding schools.

An important part of a principal's job is to weave a school's past, present, and future into a narrative that provides coherence and inspiration for teachers, students, and parents. That narrative is more powerful and effective if they use data to back up their stories.

In this chapter, principals and their mentors explore the use of data for:

- developing an all-school practice of data collection;
- giving teachers and students ownership and responsibility for collecting data that informs and facilitates their learning;
- motivating teachers and students to learn from mistakes and persevere to mastery;
- developing common understandings about what is true;
- creating a continual cycle of improvement.

Developing an All-School Practice of Data Collection

Principal: Jessica is a third year principal at Jefferson Elementary School
Mentor: Brad is a veteran principal from another school in her district

Jessica: Our faculty has moved a long way since we last talked. Teachers are more serious about their work and they're working together to improve instruction. But as we've become more passionate about our work, I've noticed our conversations increasingly devolve into the defense of cherished beliefs. One person believes in direct instruction, another in experiential learning. Neither convinces the other to question his/her beliefs. We need to measure student learning in a way that validates or refutes our belief systems. Otherwise, we just retreat into different camps and stop learning from one another.

Brad: I think it's time to talk about collecting and using data.

Jessica: I've gingerly approached that subject and met with groans and complaints about one more thing to do. I'm also afraid federal mandates have given testing and data a bad name.

Brad: I think teachers complain about something new until they see how it positively affects student learning. Most teachers I know are willing to try almost anything if they're convinced it will increase student learning.

Jessica: I suppose that's true, but how can I convince them to start collecting data, particularly those who see teaching as a God given talent and are allergic to anything smacking of regimentation.

Brad: Read and study together, then give them responsibility for collecting their own data. Data that informs their practice and enhances student learning, not data designed to judge them. A book called *Driven by Data* by Paul Bambrick-Santoyo is particularly useful.[1] You might want to start with some small study groups or a staff meeting session or two discussing parts of the book.

Jessica: I'm interested in creating a culture where decisions are made on the basis of data rather than closely held beliefs or in some cases even prejudices. How would you suggest we begin?

Using Data You Already Have

Brad: You might begin by initiating an all-staff conversation to analyze data you already have (test scores or discipline data) and then decide what additional data you need to collect to address the issues that arise from the original data. The important thing is to plan *with* teachers rather than *for* them.

The process of a group analyzing data together promotes cohesiveness, responsibility, and an increasingly sophisticated approach to instructional improvement. Remember, the end game of data collection is to improve student learning and that's more likely to happen if teachers or students feel ownership in the data they're collecting and analyzing. These discussions begin with a well-structured all-staff conversation and end with concrete individual plans for addressing the issues that surface from the data.

When our faculty first began to analyze our standardized test scores together, we discovered an interesting pattern that enabled us to greatly improve our scores. We found that many students stopped answering questions when they became difficult. So we decided to teach students about *probability and persistence.* Both concepts, we thought would serve them well throughout their lives. Since there were no points taken off for incorrect answers, we encouraged students to think through the problems that were difficult and use their best guess for answers they weren't sure about.

The *probability* of getting a right answer if they didn't answer a question at all was zero. The *probability* of getting a right answer went up as they thought through the problem and gave it their best try. We also talked about *persistence*. It's not easy to keep going when the going gets tough. But *persistence* is the essential quality in almost every successful endeavor. These important life lessons were easily woven into our regular curriculum, benefited our students, and substantially raised our test scores.

Collecting New Data

Jessica: After those initial all-staff discussions, I wonder if it might be a good idea to challenge teachers to select an area of instruction they're interested in and collect data that either confirms or refutes their assumptions about student learning in that area. I'm thinking I might actually require teachers who are being evaluated this year to conduct a small study. Nothing elaborate, just something to get them started using data to solve problems and improve instruction.

Brad: The fourth grade teacher at our school collected data that changed the way he taught math. He taught the unit on fractions the way the textbook directed. Then he divided the class into two groups being careful to include a range of students with different levels of math achievement in each group. He then had Group A complete the homework assigned by the textbook authors. He gave the students in Group B journals and had them write about what they'd learned in math that day in their own words. At the end of the unit, he gave both groups the textbook test.

The group that journaled did statistically significantly better on the textbook test than those who did the textbook suggested homework. He interpreted the data to mean that constructing their math understanding in words was more useful to students in developing an understanding of the mathematical concepts than the repetition called for in the textbook homework. After that he included journaling in almost all his math assignments. Just to be safe, he didn't entirely give up the textbook homework, but he did scale it back. He's now in the process of collecting data on using journaling in math class throughout the year.

Jessica: Interesting story … I think I'll use it to introduce our staff conversation about collecting and using data. I'll challenge teachers to ask their students to gather and graph data about their academic progress. Hopefully, the idea of collecting and using data to tell a story about progress and learning will begin to spread throughout our school.

Brad: At our school, teachers and students have discovered lots of informal ways to use data to discover what's really happening. David supervises students on the playground. He has very stringent rules and is strict about enforcing them. When a student violates a rule, he makes them sit on a bench on the side of the playground. One day an African-American student complained that David, who is white, picked on African-American kids making them sit on the bench more often than white kids. To find out if that was true, he did some informal data collection. He asked all the students who'd been told to sit on the bench during the past school year to get in one line and all the students who had never had to sit on the bench to get in another line. In a few minutes, he had visual data that settled the situation. Although both lines had African-American and white students, there were more white students in the line of those who'd been asked to sit on the bench.

David opened himself to the possibility that there might have been more African-American students in the bench line. That might mean he was paying closer attention to African-American students who broke the rules and was more lenient toward white students, or it might mean there were more African-American students who broke the rules. The data he collected didn't resolve this issue, but it did refute the complaining student's observation. David said he would continue to enforce the rules and would do a monthly data check to make sure he was being even handed in enforcing the rules. He told students he hoped the line of students who had to sit on the bench would get shorter with each passing month. The students took this as a challenge and although the line never totally disappeared, it did get shorter each month. David attributes this success to his informal collection and visual representation of data.

I have a friend Susie who teaches middle school English. She's interested in teaching her students to expresses their ideas orally and to participate intelligently in group conversations. She calls one of her teaching strategies "Freeze the Action." During a class discussion, she collects data by putting marks by a student's name when he connects his reading to something else he's experienced or read, asks a clarifying question, or makes an astute observation of the text. After the conversation has gone on for a while, Susie says, "Freeze the Action" and holds up the data she's been collecting. Then she asks the class what the data is telling them. Comments such as Joey talked a lot, Jessie asked some good questions, or Sam didn't talk much but did a good job of connecting the text to his baseball practice. Susie reports that as students become more aware of their role in the conversation, as well as the contributions of everyone else, their ability to become productive members of an intelligent group conversation rises. She doesn't have to lecture or scold, she lets the data do the teaching.

Jessica: If teachers and students are using data to explore the truth and fuel their learning, I should gather data and use it to inform my decisions as well.

Brad: Great idea. It will help you gain a better understanding of what's happening in your school. It's easy to get in the habit of listening to only the few "loud voices" who have a particular point of view or to fall into the habit of unquestioningly accepting the myths that have governed decisions in your school for a long time. Collecting data can help you see a broader and deeper truth that leads to better decisions.

Give Teachers and Students Ownership and Responsibility for Collecting Data that Informs and Facilitates Their Learning

Jessica: We've talked about ways to help teachers take responsibility for collecting and using data to inform and improve their classroom practice. I think that's a great way to begin, but I also want to talk more about having the faculty as a whole engage in data collection and analysis that affects the whole school.

Every year, the Director of Professional Development comes to a staff meeting and reviews our school's standardized test scores. She comes with a slick bound report and a PowerPoint presentation. Everyone listens politely and a few folks ask questions, but I have the feeling not many teachers are really engaging with data and I rarely notice that it has any effect on their classroom practice.

Perhaps they don't understand the data or don't know how to apply it to their practice. Perhaps they resent what they perceive as an effort to criticize and fix them. In the end, the data is either ignored, resented, or both.

Brad: We had the same problem at our school. Now our Director of Professional Development does something that helps folks engage with the data. About a week before she is scheduled to make a presentation, she sends teachers their test scores with a cover letter asking them to review the data by asking themselves the following questions:

- What is the data telling you?
- Are there any trends over time?
- What can you celebrate?

- What questions does the data raise?
- How can you find out more?
- How can you use what you've learned to improve your practice?

At the meeting, she puts large sheets of chart paper around the room with one of the questions at the top of each sheet. She gives teachers markers and asks them to go around the room and respond to the questions recording what they noticed as they reviewed their reports. If they agreed with a remark that someone else wrote, she tells them to put a check mark next to that remark. When this is complete, she asked the group to answer these questions:

- What were the most frequently raised points?
- What questions did this activity raise that we should pay attention to?
- What should we do next?

These questions helped us engage with our test data, but we realized we needed on-going conversations if the data was really going to inform and improve our practice. First, we decided to devote one or two more staff meetings to report to one another how we were using what we learned from the initial data discussion to improve our practice. These conversations have been extremely fruitful.

We used to dread getting back test scores. We were defensive and emotional rather than open and curious. Test scores seemed like a judgment of us as teachers, not tools to help us grow. We now eagerly dig into the data to see where and how we can improve. Instead of an indictment of our efforts, the data helps us tell an on-going story about the progress we're making.

Motivating Teachers and Students to Learn from Mistakes and Persevere to Mastery

Jessica: I'm interested in the relationship of data collection and motivation of both teachers and students. It seems to me we have three basic ways of evaluating and motivating folks. We:

- measure them against a standard (a student is not at grade level);
- compare them to one another (grading on a curve or class ranking);
- measure growth (keeping track of progress).

While all three systems have merit in different situations, I've found that measuring growth is the most motivating. This is particularly true for struggling students. A standard may seem far away, and a student may always fall short of his classmates, but he can learn if he maintains the effort necessary for mastery. Maintaining that effort is greatly facilitated by collecting data on progress and making it visual.

Graphing Progress. Actually, learning to measure progress toward a goal is an important life lesson for everyone. All of us eventually run into situations in which a goal seems distant and maybe even impossible to reach. Students who learn to measure progress toward that goal are more likely to have the energy and persistence to reach the goal. I can't think of a more important life lesson.

Brad: Maybe a good place to begin with your faculty would be to share what you've just told me, and ask them to help students pick an area of desired growth and measure progress toward their goal. Measuring progress and making their data visible should help even the most reluctant learners maintain the optimism and energy necessary to reach their goal.

Interim Assessments. It's also important to include one or several interim assessments so teachers and/or students can see how far they are from reaching their goal and can adjust their game plan accordingly. Paul Bambrick-Santoyo in *Driven By Data* makes a strong case for always including interim assessments.[1]

He compares the lack of interim assessments to a basketball game without a scoreboard. It's difficult to make a realistic game plan when you don't know the score. Likewise, if your goal is to make sure every student reaches the finish line, it's important they get feedback on their progress in time to correct course. When there is little or no opportunity for revision or adjustment, tests and papers are viewed as a judgment of rather than a learning opportunity. When there is only one chance to get the right answer or to express oneself clearly, mistakes become failures, and many students shut down and lose learning opportunities.

In a school that emphasizes learning rather than judgment, there are second or third chances and everyone has the opportunity to master all the material.

Interim assessments are used to find out what students have learned and to help them fill in the gaps in their learning. Data from these assessments are charted so students can see how they're growing. I've always thought it strange when teachers average interim assessments into students' final grade without giving them the opportunity to learn from their mistakes.

Jessica: That practice is leftover from the time when our goal was to sort students into groups (advanced, average, failing) rather than doing everything we could to help all students learn all the material.

Brad: You know we used to look at teacher growth the same way. We thought teachers were born, not made. A principal's job was to manage teachers, not learn with them. We didn't expect teachers to take responsibility for their own learning or, for that matter, the learning of their students. Some folks were just smarter or more energetic than others. There wasn't much a principal or teacher could do about that. Principals managed teachers and teachers managed students. Teachers were evaluated on the basis of their good intentions, hard work, personalities, or popularity rather than on what their students actually learned. We now know that collecting data about a teacher's practice and a student's progress can fuel a virtuous cycle of learning and improvement. This shifts the emphasis from what is taught to what is learned. Teachers in these schools measure progress by what students actually learn, not by what they intended to teach. I think the best way to get started is for teachers and students to identify for themselves which goals and data are important to them. Once they begin to collect individual data on their own progress, you'll want to move to measuring progress toward all-school and district goals.

Jessica: At the beginning of each school year we have conferences with students, teachers, and parents to set student goals for the year. It might be interesting to ask what kind of data the student will collect to measure his progress toward their goals. It might be as simple as "I'm going to read five non-fiction books this semester." The data is easy to collect and the goal a lot clearer and easily measured than, " I'm going to read more non-fiction books this semester." A student who struggles in math might set a goal of mastering long division or learning the times tables. He could measure progress on interim assessments.

I also have an initial conference with all the teachers I will be evaluating that year. The teacher and I work together to set goals for the year. From now on I'll ask what kind of data she needs to gather to tell her how well she is doing in moving toward her goals. In our subsequent conferences, I'll need to ask what she is learning from the data she is collecting.

Making Data Visible

Brad: They say a picture is worth a thousand words. Well, a picture of data is probably worth 10,000 words. Just think how much information is contained in a simple graph. In a flash, you can compare past and present data. You can compare to other people or situations similar to yours. Data visualization allows us to get a quick understanding of complex situations and the relationship among different data sets.

Develop Common Understandings about What is True

Jessica: Our staff conversations often devolve into philosophical debates about what is the best way to promote student learning. Many of our teachers have deep, long-held beliefs about how students learn and why they behave the way they do. These conversations, although heartfelt, rarely lead to changes or improvements in instruction. We each go back onto our own corners and teach just as we did before, convinced that our colleagues are wrong. We rarely actually learn from one another.

Brad: Data can help you unlock the energy in those debates. In a data driven school, the question quickly becomes, what data do we need to collect to decide what is true? Does practicing arithmetic algorithms in isolation increase a student's ability to solve math problems in context? Do weekly spelling tests decrease the number of incorrectly spelled words on written work? Are students from a particular background more likely to have discipline problems? Does sending students to the office or suspending them decrease or increase the number of subsequent infractions?

Jessica: I can see how that might help. But a lot of issues we face aren't so easily resolved. For example, the quality of teaching or the teacher's belief system might influence whether direct instruction or allowing students to discover for themselves produces the most learning and there might be factors other than suspension that affect student behavior.

Brad: That's true. Data collection doesn't solve every problem, but even when the evidence isn't as clear as we'd like, it can shed light on a debate. Enough light to enable the staff to develop some common understandings and learn from one another. At the very least, it can create doubt when certainty used to rule. Doubt is often the first step in learning.

Jessica: It might be interesting to ask teachers what data they need to collect to validate their point of view. Then ask them to set up a little action research project to confirm or deny their suppositions. I know this may not totally resolve complex pedagogical and behavioral issues, but it would get us looking at data and asking questions, rather than just defending our individual points of view.

Brad: It would make your faculty conversations more interesting, informative, and useful.

Creating a Continual Cycle of Improvement

Jessica: I'm beginning to understand how powerful data collection can be. I like the idea of focusing on small projects that are meaningful to individuals. But I'd also like to talk about standardized test scores. You told me how your Director of Professional Development works with teachers to help them dig into the data standardized tests provide. Now I'd like to talk about what to do after she leaves. How do we make sure we're actually using that data to improve instruction?

Brad: Excellent question. I think you're talking about a continual cycle of improvement where test scores lead to improved instruction, and improved instruction calls for the collection of new data that in turn improves instruction in a never-ending cycle of improvement.

Jessica: That's exactly what I want.

Brad: You start with an all-staff meeting asking the questions we discussed earlier.

Then ask teachers to write a plan based on what they learned from the test score data. I suggest you meet with individuals or small groups of teachers (grade levels or departments) to discuss these plans, to talk about the successes and problems they've run into and help one another adjust plans.

Unless you reach 100 percent success, you'll always be creating a virtuous cycle of improvement (data collection, improved instruction, data collection, improved instruction). Keeping track of your successes and pinpointing areas that need improvement creates a sense of positive energy and optimism that feeds on itself and fuels a continual cycle of improvement.

Your long-term goal is to create a learning culture fueled by data collection for both teachers and students. You want the virtuous cycle of identifying an issue, collecting data, selecting a solution based on the data, collecting data to evaluate progress, and adjusting instruction appropriately to permeate your school.

Conclusion

Successful principals work with teachers to collect and use data to tell the story of what children are learning, pinpoint effective ways to improve instruction, and motivate students to persist to mastery. The science of data collection married to the art of teaching results in great teaching and outstanding schools.

Strategies for Becoming a Reflective Leader

Journaling

Note two or three current projects or problems in which data collection might deepen your understanding and lead to creative solutions. Develop plans for collecting data that addresses these issues.

Review test scores and other existing data (e.g. discipline referrals). Ask yourself "What does this data tell us?" and "What solutions does the data analysis suggest?"

How might collecting data on their progress facilitate student learning?

Collective Wisdom

All-staff conversation—brainstorm individual and all-school projects or problems on which data collection might shed light. Make sure teachers know about this conversation in advance so they have time to consider various possibilities.

Give teachers the opportunity to share data collection projects they are doing with their students.

Look at existing data (e.g., test scores, discipline referrals). Ask, "What does this data tell us?" "What solutions does your analysis suggest?"

Ask teachers to share how they collect and use data to motivate students to persist to mastery.

Practicing New Behavior

Ask teachers to either create new data or use existing data to shed light on a project or problem they currently have. Do the same yourself. Use a staff meeting or meetings to share the results of these projects. You might have one or two reports at meetings over a period of time. Begin with your report. A smaller number of reports over a longer period of time allows the habit of data collection to seep more deeply into the culture.

Implement a plan that creates a virtuous cycle of continual improvement. Include the following steps:

- Collect data.
- Analyze data and make plans based on data results.
- Change behavior.
- Collect data.

Citation

1. Paul Bambrick-Santoyo, *Driven by Data: A Practical Guide to Improve Instruction* (San Francisco, CA: Jossey-Bass, 2010).

Additional Reading

Victoria Bernhardt, *Using Data to Improve Student learning in School Districts* (New York, NY: Routledge, 2006)

Kathryn Boudett, Elizabeth City, and Richard Murnane, *Data Wise: A Step-by-Step Guide to Using Assessment Results to Improve Teaching and* Learning (Cambridge, MA: Harvard Education Press, 2013).

Nancy Love, *Using Data to Improve Learning for All* (Thousand Oaks, CA: Corwin Press, 2009).

10 Improving Curriculum and Instruction

From Creating Orthodoxies to Continual Change

Tradition is a powerful anchor that keeps the complex educational enterprise called school on a steady course. But tradition can inhibit experimentation and growth. Innovation encourages fresh responses to changing conditions, but can cause disruption and confusion. When schools flit from one reform to another, there's no time for curriculum and instruction to mature. But when good ideas harden into orthodoxies, experimentation and growth come to a halt. Principals must consider all these possibilities in their role as instructional leaders.

In this chapter, principals and mentors discuss a principal's role in curriculum and instruction and ways to nurture a culture of growth and continual improvement. Their conversations focus on the following:

- creating a culture of ownership and innovation;
- starting and maintaining on-going conversations about curriculum and instruction;
- grounding curriculum and instruction in core beliefs about human development and student learning;
- change and continual growth;
- moving from private practice to collaborative teaching and learning.

Creating a Culture of Ownership and Innovation

Principal: Kyle is the new principal of Oakville Middle School
Mentor: Catherine is a retired principal assigned to Kyle as a mentor

Kyle: I'd like to talk about a principal's role in curriculum and instruction. I have teachers who know more about curriculum and instruction than I do, but seem hesitant to assume leadership roles.

I've also worked with principals who required certain instructional procedures. Although the procedures were sound, they created a culture of compliance rather than ownership and innovation. I don't want that either. How do I find balance between too little principal leadership and too much?

Catherine: It's more a matter of *what* you do than *how much* you do.

Kyle: Some teachers are waiting for me to tell them what to do. Others push against anything I suggest. A few are eager to work with their colleagues to grow their practice, but don't know how to get started. I want to find a way to help them work together and be open to innovation without the disruption that comes from adopting one new program after the other.

Catherine: Your leadership role in curriculum and instruction depends on what kind of school you want to create. Your district has adopted a curriculum, endorsed a style of instruction, and set long term and annual goals. How that curriculum and instruction are enacted in the classroom depends on the ways teachers put those programs into practice. Some principals feel it's most expedient and effective to tell teachers what to do and check to make sure they're doing what they're told. Others work with teachers to build their capacity to understand student learning and continually improve their practice, avoiding frequent lurches from one program to another.

Kyle: That's what I want to do. I've noticed that in the best schools I've visited, teachers have a strong sense of ownership and expertise in the curriculum and instructional strategies they use. How do I grow such a school?

Catherine: You begin with yourself. In schools that inspire a culture of ownership and innovation, principals are the lead learners. They eagerly participate in learning opportunities with teachers. They don't sit in the back and answer e-mail. They talk about and utilize what they've learned. There's a quote from Betty Sue Flowers, former director of the Lyndon Baines Johnson Library and Museum and Emeritus Professor of English, that guides my thinking about leadership. I don't remember the exact words, but the meaning is always with me. Leadership is less about what you do and more about what you are.

If a leader is an enthusiastic learner himself, the habit and expectation of continual improvement will become embedded in the school culture. You said there are teachers on your faculty who have greater expertise in a particular curriculum than you do. Let them take the lead in that area and you learn with the rest of the faculty. Your success as an instructional leader rests more on assuming the following roles than on your expertise in any particular area:

- A designer who uses a variety of venues to structure conversations about curriculum and instruction.
- An inspiration who uses outside experts, readings, quotes, written teacher evaluations, and story telling to challenge and inspire continual improvement.
- A nurturer who helps teachers work through the inevitable difficulties of growth and uses mistakes and problems as opportunities for learning.
- A standard bearer who sets high standards, and holds himself and teachers to them. Maintains a clear and consistent focus on individual student learning and asks questions that connect big ideas to everyday events in classrooms.
- A learner who becomes the school's lead learner by enthusiastically and fully participating in professional development activities and frequently refers to her learning and tells stories about student and teacher learning.

Starting and Maintaining On-Going Conversations about Curriculum and Instruction

Kyle: Let's talk about the designer part.

Catherine: Establish an expectation of continual growth. Talk with teachers about problems and mistakes as opportunities for growth and constantly push for deeper understanding and more sophisticated skills for yourself and teachers.

It's often simple basic questions that elicit the deepest thinking.

- What have you tried?
- What was the result?
- How do you know?
- What will you do next?
- What concerns you?
- What else do you need?

One of the best principals I've known is a master at talking about big pedagogical ideas, zooming in to the concrete details of classroom practice that bring those ideas to life, then zooming back to the big ideas. Asking questions that connect everyday classroom activities to larger pedagogical ideas help teachers deepen their understanding and improve their practice.

Initiate and support a variety of on-going conversations about curriculum and instruction throughout the school and throughout the school year. These conversations should take place in all-faculty meetings, smaller groups (e.g. grade level, department or PLCs), and individual talks with you or with colleagues or mentors. I've found these conversations to be most effective when they are grounded in concrete artifacts.

Kyle: For example?
Catherine: It might be

- student work;
- written observations of teachers or students by the principal or colleagues;
- books or articles;
- information gleaned from conferences;
- review of the curriculum in light of specific student needs;
- test scores;
- videos of teachers teaching lessons.

Teachers are busy people. Time they have for reflection is precious. It's your job to create time and space for these conversations and make certain they actually improve what happens in classrooms. I've found that grounding conversations in artifacts provides the discipline that keeps them focused and productive. You might ask teachers to bring written work or test scores from students who are struggling to a small meeting of colleagues or an all-staff meeting that breaks into smaller groups. Then have groups work together to analyze the artifacts and help one another make plans for future instruction.

Your school should be abuzz with serious and practical talk about how to best design, deliver, and adjust curriculum and instruction to meet students' needs. This takes a lot of planning and a serious commitment to protecting the time and space for these conversations.

Kyle: That sounds great, but our agendas are already full. I don't think we have time for that kind of talk.

Catherine: It might be interesting to notice what actually gets talked about at meetings and individual conferences. In a lot of schools, meeting time is used for planning events, discussing logistic issues, or making announcements. This is a waste of the two most precious resources schools have for improvement ... time to think and learn together and the collective wisdom and thinking of teachers. If you want to build a faculty that's serious about constantly improving instruction, you have to find time for them to talk together. This means all (or at least the large majority) of meetings and individual conferences are reserved for serious talk about curriculum and instruction. Find other venues for planning and dispersing information.

Kyle: That won't be easy. But I like that you're not suggesting any additional meetings, just redefining the meetings we already have. Teachers will like that too.

This will shift how I spend my time. I'll need to spend more time sitting in on PLCs, grade level, and department meetings. When I meet with teachers I'm evaluating, I think I'll ask them to bring student work, observations of other teachers, test scores, etc. for us to discuss.

I'll ask new teachers to observe more experienced teachers and discuss with the experienced teacher and me what they saw. This will give them the opportunity to ask the observed teacher why she made certain decisions. The conversation should bump up everyone's game.

I'll also ask them to bring work from a student who's struggling, who's on track, and who's advanced for us to discuss.

Catherine: That's a great place to begin. You may experience some pushback at the beginning. Teachers aren't always comfortable observing one another, but if you make it clear that the point of the observation is to learn from, not judge, one another and you give the idea time to ripen I think you'll find teacher-to-teacher observations a powerful learning tool for everyone. The important thing is not to quit because you get some pushback. It may take a while.

Kyle: You've given me a lot to think about. I've taken some writing courses. The advice they always give is to show, not tell. I think that's what you're suggesting I do to build a growing, thoughtful faculty. Instead of telling teachers what to do, you're suggesting we study and work together to grow our collective expertise.

Catherine: Exactly, I'll be eager to hear how these conversations go.

Kyle: I love the idea of engaging the faculty in meaningful conversations about curriculum and instruction. But, those conversations are liable to take some time before they yield results. Unfortunately, we don't have the luxury of time. The district folks are telling us our test scores need to improve right away, particularly our math scores.

I used to teach math and have some specific ideas about what we might do to close the gaps our standardized test scores revealed. But I'm reluctant to be too prescriptive. I want our teachers to become thoughtful professionals who own the curriculum, not cogs in a machine who obey me.

Catherine: No system is perfect. While I like the idea of learning with teachers rather than telling them what to do, there are times when insisting on certain instructional procedures might be necessary. However, as matters improve, I'd move away from ordering and inspecting to learning and improving together. Sometimes whole schools or school districts are in such trouble that an ordering and inspection approach is the best option, at least at the beginning. But if you want to create an engaged and thoughtful faculty, I'd move away from that approach as soon instruction begins to improve. In the long run, I think learning together produces the strongest and most successful pedagogy.

Kyle: How should we begin?

Grounding Innovation in Core Beliefs about Curriculum and Instruction

Catherine: You might begin by helping the faculty examine the belief systems on which their current pedagogy rests. You could use system thinking tools such as the "Iceberg" (Figure 10.1) and "Ladder of Inference" (Figure 10.2) to unearth and examine the beliefs that underlie their current curriculum and instructional decisions.

Next help teachers commit to some common beliefs about learning and teaching. Brainstorming and dot voting can help with this endeavor. Once these core beliefs are established, give teachers opportunities to question whether current curricular and instructional decisions are true to these beliefs. For example, many faculties list "All children can learn" as a core value. But careful examination of actual instructional practices often reveals a weak commitment to this belief.

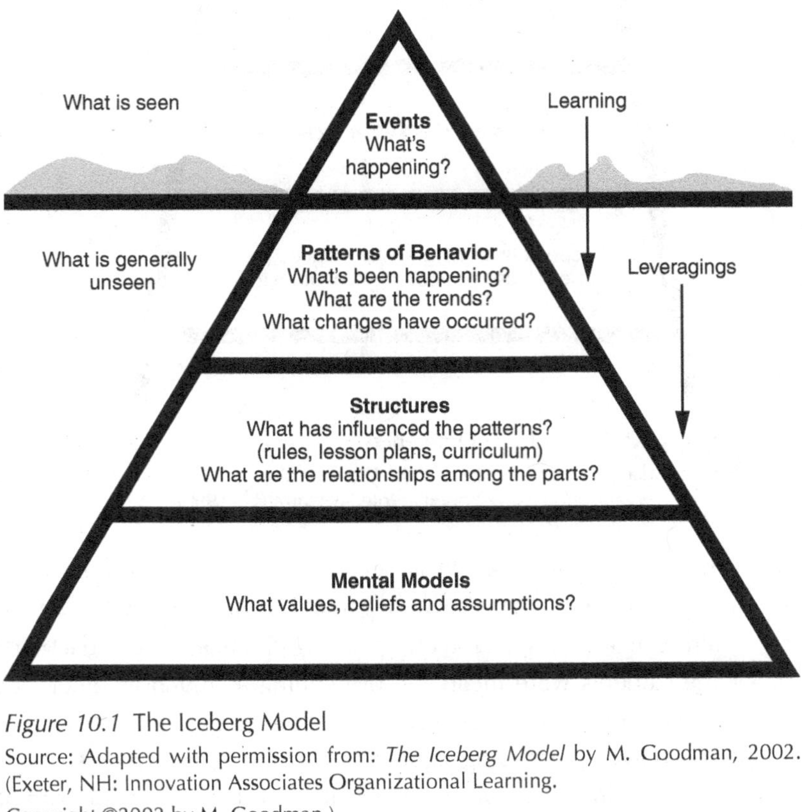

Figure 10.1 The Iceberg Model

Source: Adapted with permission from: *The Iceberg Model* by M. Goodman, 2002. (Exeter, NH: Innovation Associates Organizational Learning. Copyright ©2002 by M. Goodman.)

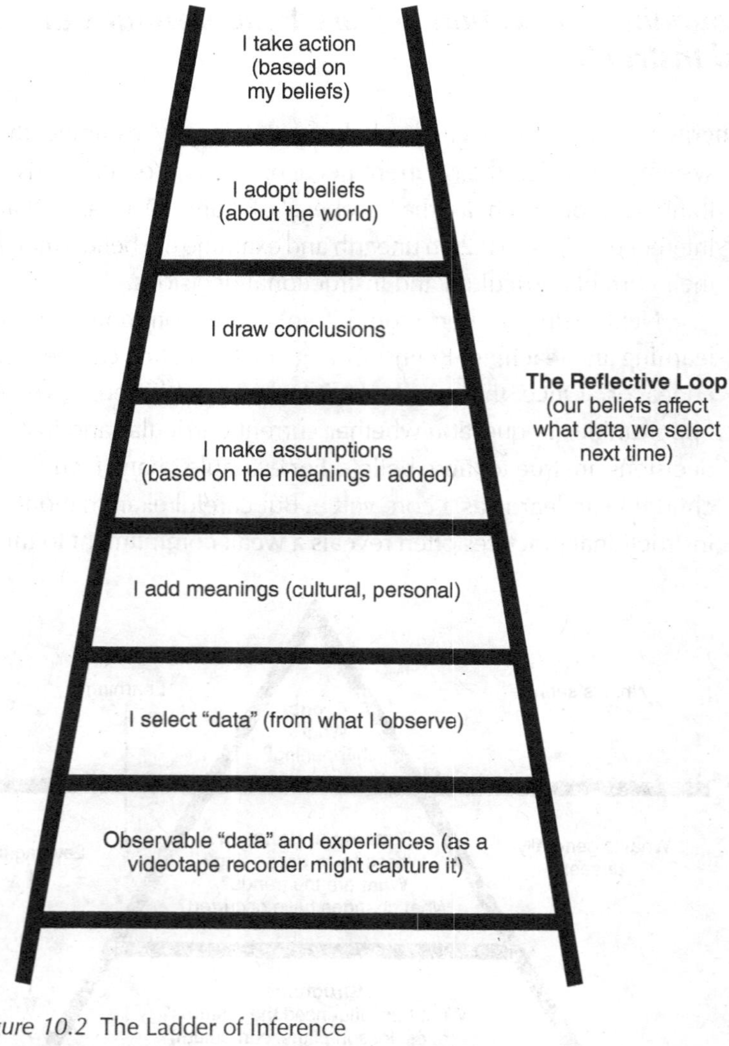

Figure 10.2 The Ladder of Inference

Source: Adapted from: Peter M. Senge, *The Fifth Discipline: The Art and Practice of The Learning Organization* (New York: Doubleday/Currency, 1990).

When I arrived at Oakville students were divided into "ability groups" for reading instruction. As we began to examine our beliefs about how children learn, we realized our grouping practices reflected a belief that some students were incapable of learning as much as other students and we were able to identify those students at a very early age. We decided to stop grouping students by what we perceived as ability and begin teaching based on our beliefs that all students could learn all the material. We also believed that labeling students by putting them in a particular group could be detrimental to their ability and desire to learn.

Our examination of how our practices related to our beliefs led us to make changes in how we grouped students. This, in turn, caused us to question how we sequenced curriculum. One reform led to another as we worked to make our practice consistent with our beliefs. Our beliefs were also changing as we read, observed, and talked with one another.

We've talked before about Paul Shaw's book *Taking Charge: Leading with Passion and Purpose in the Principalship.*[1] He has a wonderful chapter on "The Principal and the Curriculum." He says, "I have shown that the principal needs to have a significant role in the school's curriculum—a curriculum that is not so much a deliverable product but, rather, a guide that enables us to proactively design, plan, and reflect on improving the learning experience and life chances of all our pupils." He also says, "principals and teachers need to dialogue and act together based on their own best-educated understanding of how people internalize and apply new information and perform new operations."

Kyle: That sounds great, but in the end, I'll be held responsible for implementing the district curriculum and promoting quality instruction. I don't know how much leeway I should give teachers.

Catherine: It *is* your job to implement the district curriculum and promote quality instruction, but it's been my experience that when you and teachers become partners in this endeavor, they become thoughtful and sophisticated professionals. This doesn't happen when all you expect is adherence to preset values and procedures. It takes more time, but in the end, you have a smarter, more committed, and more effective faculty. *Principals form a partnership with teachers when they stop telling and start asking questions.*

- Lexi seemed distracted and didn't participate in the conversation. What's going on?
- What are your plans for engaging Lexi?

This doesn't mean you give up control. You simply expand the conversation to include everyone. Although your voice is now one among many, it's still the most powerful voice. But now you have the collective wisdom and commitment of the entire faculty.

Once a set of common beliefs is established, look at the specifics of the curriculum and instruction to see how the details of what actually goes on in the classroom match your beliefs. Examination of our beliefs caused us to change the way we grouped students. I have a friend at a nearby middle school that changed the way they graded student work as a result of examining their beliefs. Teachers at his school no longer include interim test scores in a student's final grade. Interim tests, they decided, were to help students understand how much they already knew and how much more they needed to learn. If they mastered the material at the end of the course, it seemed counter-productive to average the interim score into the final score.

Kyle: I have two questions. What did you discuss at small group meetings? How did you keep track of what was happening?

Catherine: Sometimes our conversations focused on how to deliver the curriculum to particular students or group of students. As we talked about individual students, a case study approach evolved. We developed a simple template for a teacher to complete and used the information she provided to focus our conversations. Sometimes they were students who struggled, other times, students who were advanced. Although we focused on a single student or small group of students, our case studies taught us a lot about all our students.

In order to keep our meetings focused and productive, I asked teachers who ran them to e-mail me and other members of the team their agendas. This kept the conversation focused and purposeful. The agendas didn't have to be formal, but they did need to include the topic or topics to be discussed and any outside reading or other resources that might inform the conversation.

I tried to attend as many meetings as possible. I gave them priority on my schedule. I explained my purpose was to allow me to share in their learning, not to check up on them. As I spent time in these meetings, I gained a new respect for the growing knowledge and wisdom of our faculty. My role changed from telling teachers what to do, to asking the kind of questions that helped them think deeply about their practice. Usually these were simple questions such as:

- How do you know?
- What do you expect to happen?
- How will you know?
- What else do you need to know?
- How can we help you?

We were no longer independent contractors working behind closed doors. We were now a team working together to improve instruction for all our students. Initially I gave up some power, but in the end I gained a much more powerful faculty.

Continual On-going Learning and Improvement vs. Jumping from One "Perfect Solution" to Another

Kyle: I'm afraid some of our teachers are just too burned out to try anything new. They've had two superintendents and three principals in the past five years. Each new administrator wanted to make his/her mark and brought in new ideas about curriculum and instruction. Teachers never had time to master one before a new set of ideas was introduced. Many of the ideas were great, but the constant changing was a problem.

Even if we stick with the same curriculum and instruction for a while, there's always a push to see results quickly and a rush to make adjustments before the new ideas have time to ripen. Each new curriculum promises to boost our test scores. Eventually, because there are no perfect solutions, because the program isn't fully implemented, or because there isn't time to work out all the kinks, the program fails and a new program is adopted causing disruption, frustration, and cynicism. These frequent changes mean teachers never have time to deepen their understanding of a particular curriculum and make the many small adjustments that bring a curriculum to maturity. The cost of this constant change is measured in wasted time, money, and teachers' optimism and good will.

Catherine: I'm not sure how much control you actually have over district wide decisions, but you can certainly speak up about the damage these constant changes cause, no matter how well intentioned. Also, if you've established a variety of venues for teachers to talk with one another about their work, you have a built-in way to become familiar with the new curriculum and adjust it to the values and culture of your school.

Teachers who are expected to move from one program to another that is not firmly grounded in their own beliefs about how students learn, nor are given the time and support to make the new curriculum their own, become burned out and cynical ... not a good recipe for an outstanding school.

There are also schools with the opposite problem. Once transformational ideas have over time been allowed to become new orthodoxies that are impervious to change. Schools that have established a set of guiding principles for how students learn, many on-going venues for conversations about curriculum and instruction, and the expectation of continual growth provide an antidote for both the problem of frequent disruptive changes and hardened orthodoxies in curriculum and instruction.

Change and Continual Growth

Kyle: I think the reason we keep changing curriculum is we believe if we only find the right program it will enable us to raise our test scores and meet the learning needs of all our students. Then we'll be able to relax and enjoy the fruits of our labor. What I hear you saying is

- there is no perfect program;
- we have to continually study, evaluate, and grow our curriculum and instruction;
- there will be no end point and no relaxing.

Catherine: I know it sounds exhausting. My experience is the opposite. Participating in a learning community that's alive with inquiry and exploration in pursuit of a noble cause is energizing and exciting.

Along with creating venues for serious discussion about curriculum and instruction, I underscored the expectation of continuous learning and growth by mentioning teachers' learning and growth in their evaluations. I didn't expect them to be perfect, but I did expect teachers to be scholars of student learning and apply what they learned to their students. I mentioned teachers' participation in learning activities, growth in pedagogy, and improved student learning in their evaluations. This got their attention and provided the incentive and support they needed to continue learning and improving their practice.

Teachers were working harder than ever, but they were pumped about what they were learning. Fear that they might make a mistake was replaced by the excitement of reaching more students and the freedom to explore new ideas. The isolation of the classroom was replaced by the support and challenge of colleagues. It was an amazing transformation. Instead of adding new ideas one by one, knowledge, understanding, and expertise were growing exponentially. A new energy and optimism pervaded our work.

Kyle: This sounds exciting and a bit daunting. It's hard to know where to begin.

Catherine: Do you remember when we first started working together, I told you about my Zoysia grass metaphor for how deep cultural change often takes place?

Kyle: I love that metaphor. I assume you mean we don't have to do everything all at once. We put in plugs as the need arises and as long as we keep watering them and keep putting in new plugs, we'll develop a strong culture that chokes out the practices that are inefficient and inconsistent with our beliefs about learning.

Catherine: Exactly! Another interesting thing about this metaphor is that the need for a new plug often begins with a problem, usually a knotty one. Instead of just trying to fix the problem, mine it to see what it can teach you about your current practice and what may need changing. It's the path to continual growth and improvement.

Moving from Private Practice to Collaborative Teaching and Learning

Catherine: The principal doesn't have to be, or indeed shouldn't be the only one putting in "plugs."

An important element of a school with the expectation of continuous learning is a move from teaching as private practice to teaching as a collaborative endeavor. Schools are usually awash with knowledge and wisdom teachers have obtained from study and years of experience. In many schools there are few opportunities to unlock that knowledge and wisdom and share it throughout the school. The kinds of conversations we've been talking about provide opportunities and expectations that teachers will share information and insights and support one another's learning. As a result, the skill level of the entire faculty multiplies exponentially.

Kyle: I'm excited about putting more plugs in our lawn. Any suggestions about where to begin?

Catherine: Initiating conversations about beliefs about student learning and making plans to better align practices with beliefs would be a plug in your lawn. Let's see where that leads you. Then we'll know what the next plug should be.

I think you also need to keep in mind the leadership roles a principal as instructional leader needs to assume ... designer, inspiration nurturer, standard bearer, and lead learner. Why don't you do some journaling about your experience with these roles for us to discuss when we meet next month?

Conclusion

As instructional leaders, principals must grapple with the issues of too little or too much disruption and too little or too much top-down direction. By creating the expectation of continual improvement; a culture of ownership, responsibility, and innovation; and moving teachers from private practice to collaborative learning and planning, principals provide the scaffolding that leads to skilled teaching and sophisticated learning.

Strategies for Becoming a Reflective Leader

Journaling/Mentoring

Create a T-chart. On one side document teacher behaviors that indicate they feel ownership for curriculum and instruction and responsibility for innovations to better meet their students' needs. On the other side document behaviors that indicate teachers feel little personal responsibility for the curriculum and are mostly focused on complying with decisions someone else has made.

Think about opportunities your interactions with teachers afford for creating an expectation of continual improvement. How might you structure these conversations to help teachers view their professional development as an on-going quest for more and better ways to engage students and promote continual learning?

Talk with mentor or teacher team about the observations your journaling uncovered and work to develop a plan for shifting more ownership and responsibility for curriculum and instruction to teachers.

Create a T-chart. On one side record teacher private practice behaviors, on the other collaborative teaching opportunities and behaviors.

Collective Wisdom

What venues are currently in place for teachers to have serious substantive conversations about curriculum and instruction?

How might you arrange additional opportunities for these conversations?

Are current curriculum and instruction conversations focused and productive? What do you and teachers need to learn to make these conversations more effective and efficient in improving classroom practice?

Work with teachers to develop the time, structure, and expectations they need to engage in on-going focused and productive conversations to continually improve their classroom practice. This might include topics such as scheduling, using artifacts to ground curriculum and instruction conversations, and conducting more focused and productive meetings.

Provide a variety of venues and expectations for teachers to meet and have serious and focused curriculum and instruction that directly impacts their work with students

Provide many opportunities for teachers to exchange ideas with colleagues. Make it clear that these opportunities are cooperative efforts to help one another with the inevitable problems that accrue from and are essential for continual growth. Your attitude towards mistakes and problems as opportunities for growth rather than failures will be key in establishing a safe collaborative atmosphere.

Make certain all your conversations with teachers reflect an attitude about challenges and mistakes as opportunities for growth.

Practicing New Behaviors

Regularly participate in a variety of teacher meetings. Note how comfortable teachers feel sharing their difficulties, the kind of feedback they receive, and how effectively and efficiently teachers use this meeting time to directly impact their work with students.

When problems arise, arrange forums for teachers to share their experience and expertise and the expectation that locked in problems are often the keys to raising the bar for teachers and student learning.

Citation

1. Paul Shaw, *Taking Charge: Leading With Passion and Purpose in the Principalship* (New York, NY: Teachers College Press, 2012).

Additional Reading

Barbara Kohm and Beverly Nance, *Principals Who Learn: Asking the Right Questions Seeking the Best Solutions* (Alexandria, VA: Association for Supervision and Curriculum Development, 2007).

David Stewart, Tom Prebble, and Peter Duncan, *The Reflective Principal: Leading the School Development Process* (Katonah, NY: Richard C. Owen Publishers, 1997).